CHANGING WORLDS

CHANGING WORLDS

ROBIN GILL

T&T CLARK
A Continuum imprint
LONDON • NEW YORK

T&T CLARK LTD

A Continuum imprint

59 George Street
Edinburgh EH2 2LQ
Scotland
www.tandtclark.co.uk

370 Lexington Avenue
New York 10017–6503
USA
www.continuumbooks.com

First published 2002

ISBN 0 567 08875 8 (Paperback)
ISBN 0 567 08886 3 (Hardback)

British Library Cataloguing-in-Publication Data
A catalogue record for this book is available from the British Library

Typeset by Fakenham Photosetting Ltd, Fakenham, Norfolk NR21 8NN
Printed and bound in Great Britain by Biddles Ltd, Guildford and King's Lynn

Contents

Contents

Introduction:
Theology after September 11

A dominant concern of mine for some time has been the implications of a fast-changing world for Christian faith and practice. An overwhelming impression from travelling widely in the Anglican Communion is that change is the experience of churches everywhere. There are immense moral challenges, raising crucial issues within a fast-changing world, which are felt in every country visited . There are anxieties about churchgoing decline in many so-called Western countries and, conversely, claims about rapid church growth in a number of non-Western countries. And there is extensive bewilderment about changes in theological education. How should Christians respond to these changes? The studies presented in this book – some entirely new but others published elsewhere in earlier forms – all seek to respond to this question.

The complete manuscript of *Changing Worlds* was sent to T&T Clark at the end of August 2001. It was time then to start a sabbatical project on *Healing and Christian Ethics*. And then September 11 happened. Such a traumatic example of changing worlds clearly requires some response, even if it is extremely provisional. As I write now (in early November 2001) the war is Afghanistan is still being fought. Yet how can I possibly ignore this shattering event? So I have made some changes to the original manuscript, risky though they undoubtedly are, especially to chapter 2 on the ethics of the arms trade. The earlier version of this chapter was first published in December 2000 but it would have been irresponsible simply to leave it in its original form.

Once a greater perspective is possible it will be important to address the theme of theology after September 11 properly. This is not an event that Christian theologians can simply ignore. On the contrary, I am convinced that it adds a sharp new dimension to responsible theology – it is a *kairos* moment. For the present, however, all that I can do is attempt tentatively to draw out relevant points from the studies that follow, hoping that they may be developed further in the near future.

One of the most disturbing features of September 11 for a theologian is that it seems, at first sight, to have a religious cause. That is to say, strong Islamic beliefs have been expressed by al-Qaeda, and copies of the Koran were apparently found among the possessions of those who flew two aircraft into the towers of the World Trade Centre. The whole event apparently offers striking evidence for Richard Dawkins' contention that 'religion causes wars by generating certainty'. In the final chapter of this book I look at David Martin's 1997 study *Does Christianity Cause War?* in which he takes Dawkins to task. Martin argues: 'In one way ... the statement is irrefutable because there certainly have been wars where religion played a role. In another way it is indefensible since there certainly have been wars where religion has played no role whatever.'[1] Martin also points out that New Testament Christianity hardly supports a bellicose position. In the context of September 11 he might have made a similar point about Islam: the Koran, properly understood, hardly supports the killing of some five thousand civilians in the World Trade Centre.

At this level, Martin's argument is compelling. Wars are conducted for a variety of ideological motives – some religious and some not – and even those that are religiously based may be founded upon a serious distortion of a particular religion's basic tenets. For a sociologist nurtured upon both Weber and Durkheim there is no contradiction in holding that religion can be dysfunctional as well as functional. If Durkheim suggested how religion could provide social cohesion, Weber showed how it could also be socially disruptive. Or to take another example, discussed in chapter 6, José Casanova's influential book *Public Religions in the Modern World* has pointed afresh to the political significance of religion in the modern world. Much to the surprise of sociologists reared upon classical theories of secularization (shared by both Weber and Durkheim), the late twentieth century and now the early twenty-first century have seen some startling and unexpected examples of resurgent forms of religious fundamentalism playing a major role in shaping political realities. This was not

---

[1] David Martin, *Does Christianity Cause War?* (Oxford: Clarendon Press, 1997), p. 23.

supposed to have happened. Yet obviously it has happened. The Iranian Revolution of 1979 was largely unpredicted by scholars brought up upon classical theories of secularization. Some scholars at the time were disturbed by this, but others soon predicted that Islamic revival was a passing phenomenon. A generation later it appears to be anything but passing. As a result, the conventional wisdom that religion within the modern world can survive only in privatized forms has rapidly been replaced with Dawkins' mantra that 'religion causes wars by generating certainty'.

David Martin is surely correct in holding that this new mantra is indeed historically selective. Taking stock of the appalling examples of genocide in the twentieth century, many would argue that among the most culpable agents were Stalin, Hitler, Mao and Pol Pot – hardly a list that gives much support to the mantra. Each of the four was given to ideological certainty, and some to the certainty of atheism, but none to religious certainty.

Yet that is still not the end of the argument. September 11 apparently *was* characterized by religious certainty, at least by the perpetrators, and was even depicted as an Islamic war of defence against a crusading Christianity by Osama Bin Laden. Of course this latter charge was immediately rejected by most Western political leaders. Nevertheless, September 11 joins other world events, ranging from Northern Ireland to Israel, that have indisputably religious connotations and in which the fault lines of religion can clearly be seen. Without claiming that all wars are caused by religious certainty or that such certainty properly represents any of the religions that have been associated with modern wars, it is clear that some forms of strongly held religion can add extremely dangerous elements to conflict in the modern world. This *should* be a matter of deep concern for theologians. In that respect Dawkins is right.

If this final point is taken seriously, then there is I believe an important and urgent task for modern theologians. We must take more seriously than hitherto the negative consequences (however unintended) of religious beliefs and practices. It is not sufficient to examine religious beliefs and practices in their benign forms. Nor is it sufficient to analyse theological concepts in the ways that theologians themselves typically do. Rather we need to pay more attention to popular perceptions of religious beliefs and practices, to the ways theological concepts have been transmitted among non-theologians and to their unintended and sometimes malign consequences within society at large. This Weberian perspective lies at the heart of the first chapter in this book, *Changing Worlds*. The agenda here is set by Lynn White's critique of Christian theology for indirectly fostering a culture that has been deeply destructive of the environment. Although I reach the conclusion that this particular thesis is probably too sweeping, it does still raise important issues that have all too often been ignored by theologians. In particular, it raises a sharp question about the negative cultural effects of some forms of theology.

Even if the mantra 'religion causes wars by generating certainty' is only partly true it should worry theologians. Religious fundamentalism in the modern world should be a matter of deep theological concern. Twelve years ago, seeking to understand what fundamentalism is and why it can be so destructive, I wrote in *Competing Convictions* as follows:

> Two general features of fundamentalism might be isolated – the first cognitive and the second sociological. At a cognitive level, fundamentalism can be seen as a series of movements committed to scriptural absolutism. And, at a sociological level, it can be seen as a series of counter-cultures, that is, as movements consciously opposed to the pluralism and relativism that appear to accompany modernity. In fundamentalism these two features are intimately related: scriptural absolutism is upheld as a counter to modernity and defines the varying counter-cultural forms that fundamentalism, assumes.[2]

Whether these forms are Christian, Jewish or Muslim, on this understanding of fundamentalism they are all characterized by these two features. The certainty of scriptural absolutism becomes a means of opposing modern society. In the instance of radical fundamentalism this can involve and has involved the use of force and violence. I also noted at the time that 'counter-cultural scriptural absolutism is so antithetical to the presumptions that predominate in Western

---

[2] See my *Competing Convictions* (London: SCM Press, 1989), p. 22.

scholarship, that the Shi'ite revolution in Iran in 1979 and the political role of the Moral Majority in the American elections in the 1980s are only slowly being adequately assessed'.[3] Ironically the last decade has seen the rise of a much more sophisticated form of religious 'certainty' in the form of postmodern theological movements such as that of Radical Orthodoxy. The latter is certainly not based upon scriptural absolutism, but it has been variously depicted as 'sectarian', 'exclusivist' or 'hermetic'. Whichever label is finally judged to be most apposite, there is a dangerous combination here of a radical rejection of modernity with sharp, dogmatic and particularist theological claims.

In contrast, in the third part of this book, *Changing Worlds*, I explore those forms of recent theology that attempt to move beyond confessionalism. I was invited to give the contents of chapter 8 at a conference in South Korea in May 2001. The setting was the Presbyterian College and Theological Seminary in Seoul. With some 2500 students and 48 full-time academics, almost all with American or European doctorates, this is now one of the most impressive theological colleges in the world. The theme of the conference was theological education in the twenty-first century. Throughout, it also recognized both the changes that are manifestly taking place in moral perceptions within churches worldwide and the new situation in South Korea of churchgoing decline or stagnation. Of course we knew nothing of September 11. Nevertheless, there was an awareness among some of the speakers that the new century would require a more sensitive and less dogmatic approach to theology. This conference illustrated well how the three areas of change discussed in this book are interrelated. Indeed, the changes in theological education within the West may result in part from a decline in church ordinands studying theology and a growth of students interested in religious issues but without formal Christian commitments themselves. These changing students, in turn, seem to have brought different moral perceptions and convictions, some of them very challenging for Christian ethics. Set in the new context of September 11 it is possible that theology within the academy will become more

[3] *Competing Convictions*, p. 23.

significant, if only academic theologians can learn to move beyond dogmatic confessionalism.

The theme of the second section of this book relates more loosely to September 11. It begins with a very localized case-study, looking at church decline in Bromley and Kent during the twentieth century. It next compares the different reactions of sociologists of religion and officials within the Church of England to similar empirical evidence from other places in Britain. Then it uses three international case-studies to test the conditions in which churchgoing might still be able to grow even within the modern world. These three case-studies are all the products of my travel: first visiting and preaching in the Pro-Cathedral in Malta, secondly visiting Christians in Beijing and Xian, and thirdly preaching and lecturing on two separate visits to South Korea.

Yet there is still some link here to September 11. At a very crude level, some commentators have drawn a sharp contrast between resurgent Islam and declining Western Christianity. Such a crude contrast is of course double-edged. Some will understand it to mean that Islam might eventually triumph. They, in turn, will be divided between those who applaud this and those who are appalled by it. Others will see this as a contrast between credulous immigrant communities and the sophisticated indigenous West. In contrast, the studies in this second section of *Changing Worlds* will suggest that the growth and decline of institutional Christianity (and perhaps of Islam too) is considerably more complex than any of these crude predictions envisage. Again, it is often suggested that it is religious certainty that causes church growth – for good or ill – and a lack of certainty that causes decline. Here, too, these studies may raise other possibilities. Finally, it is sometimes supposed that church growth is incompatible with cultural pluralism. The case-study from Beijing may suggest otherwise.

This book adopts throughout both sociological and theological methods. Those who know my other writings will be aware that this is no accident. It reflects a conviction that theologians should pay careful attention to things as they are and could be before pronouncing upon things as they ought to be. A concern for theological issues which simply ignores the empirical, or projections based upon empirical data, is finally unhelpful. David Martin has long been an ally and mentor here, so it is appropriate that the final chapter examines his crucial contribution to a disciplined use of sociology within theology. His strong (and, sometimes, conservative) theological and liturgical convictions shine through his various works. The suspicion that so many theologians have that any use of sociology by them would inevitably result in social relativism or reductionism manifestly does not apply to him. He is a professional sociologist who, over many years, has shown just how important sociology can be for theological and ecclesiastical realism.

As already mentioned, some of the chapters in *Changing Worlds* have appeared elsewhere in earlier forms and all have been tested in one conference or another. Such testing, and the critical comments gained from it, are invaluable. I am most grateful to both church and university colleagues around the world for all their criticisms (whether or not I always gave the impression – as I certainly should – of actually appreciating them at the time!). The first chapter is the text of the Gore Lecture given at the kind invitation of the Dean and Chapter at Westminster Abbey. It was an added honour that David Martin was himself a Gore Lecturer (as I mention in the final chapter). An earlier version of the second chapter was first published in the *Cambridge Companion to Christian Ethics*, which I edited for Cambridge University Press in 2000. An earlier version of chapter 4 first appeared in *A Church for the 21st Century*, edited by Robert Hannaford for Gracewing in 1998. The substance of chapter 5 was first published in *Kent in the 20th Century*, edited by Nigel Yates for Boydell Press in 2001. Chapter 9 was first commissioned for the journal *Contact* in 1998 and chapter 10 was first published in *Religion and Society: Essays in Honour of David Martin*, edited by Andrew Walker and Martyn Percy for Sheffield Academic Press in 2000.

Family and church community remain as important for me as ever, despite the broad patterns of institutional decline mapped out in the chapters that follow. Coping with changing worlds is so much easier with the bedrock of both a loving family and a worshipping congregation. Although this bedrock changes, as family members die and a new generation is born and as old houses are sold and new homes and churches found, the continuities of faithful love and worship remain. Personally I cannot imagine life without this bedrock and fear for those who imagine it to be dispensable. I am grateful for this beyond words.

PART ONE

Changing Moral Perceptions

Religion and the Environment

(The Charles Gore Lecture at Westminster Abbey, November 1998)

The environment has become one of the major moral issues of our time. At the end of the second millennium, it is increasingly obvious that human beings are set on a path of unprecedented environmental destruction and that a profound moral and spiritual change is now needed. Human over-population and over-consumption have resulted in appalling pollution, soil erosion, deforestation and species extinction. More debatably, human beings may also be responsible for ozone depletion and global warming. We desperately need to change. We desperately need a change of spirit. The environmental debate is as much about religion and morality as it is about science.

All of this came home to me starkly in a visit my wife and I made to the Transkei five years ago. We stayed with the Bishop of Umzimvubu, Geoff Davies, and his family. He suggested cautiously that we might like to go with him on a day's journey to one of the remotest parts of his diocese. When he discovered that we had spent a year in a remote part of Papua New Guinea in the early 1970s along with our two young babies, he stopped being cautious. We could survive quite happily without electricity and running water. In fact we enjoy escaping from the comforts of the North for a while and love visiting remote rural communities in different parts of the world. In the event, the parishioners in the Transkei villages we visited made us enormously welcome. They seemed genuinely pleased to see visitors and were astonishingly generous to us. To our embarrassment, the local Anglican priest and his wife insisted upon moving out of their bedroom for the night to let us use it instead. Even the bishop was not given as much hospitality. The next morning they brought us a bowl of hot water to wash in and breakfast in bed. Then, in the middle of the afternoon, we joined their special feast of chicken and potatoes. We also took part in the longest service I have ever attended. For seven hours the huge congregation sang and swayed, clapped and prayed together. The liturgy seemed to include almost everything apart from an ordination service.

Transkei in May can be quite cold at night, but during the day the clear skies and weak sun bathe the countryside in a glorious yellow light. Compared with the litter-strewn squatter settlements we had seen in many urban parts of Southern Africa, rural Transkei really did seem idyllic. Unfortunately, Geoff Davies opened our eyes to a different vision. He is one of the most dedicated environmentalists in the Anglican Communion. It is hardly surprising that he was one of the first to enrol for the environment group when the Lambeth Conference met (in August 1998). On the journey home from the Transkei he stopped his car and asked us to get out and listen to the wildlife. We did as he said, but could hear only the wind. Then he told us that almost every mammal larger than a mouse, as well as most birds, had been hunted to the point of extinction. Human beings in this once ecologically vibrant part of the Transkei, together with their domestic chickens which we had enjoyed eating, now had complete dominion. Their rivals had been eliminated. Today, small boys still go on hunting trips . . . but now they are looking for the mice.

We often think that environmental destruction is a product of urban, industrial society. Of course a large part of it is. Driving on one of the endless, featureless freeways in Southern California it is easy to see this. However, what we found so shocking in this remote part of the Transkei is that rural people can also be so voracious and so unaware of their own destruction of the environment. This environmentally conscious bishop was at a loss to know how to get his own parishioners to look beyond their rural poverty at the environmental destruction that now surrounded them. It is one of the extraordinary myths of our time that country dwellers all care for the countryside they apparently love. Sadly this seems to be true of neither the rural poor nor the rural rich. It is often the rural poor in the world who suffer from environmental degradation most directly. Deforestation and agricultural pollution affect them at first hand. Yet the rural poor can be as careless of the environment as the rest of us. It is not simply their poverty that causes them to be neglectful of their environment. That much, at least, we learned from our visit.

I believe that there are profound religious issues involved in all of this. These issues are both negative and positive. Negatively, there is very real fear that religious faith can (unwittingly) contribute to environmental destruction. Some forms of religious faith may have carelessly encouraged the sort of 'dominion' of human beings over their environment so evident in our visit to the Transkei. On the other hand, positively, there is a growing awareness that it is religious faith which has sufficient power to change people's hearts and behaviour across the globe. The people we visited are a deeply religious people who take their faith seriously. Perhaps this faith, directed aright, could be a powerful factor in moving people away from heedless environmental destruction.

Of course, both of these claims need to be treated critically. There is already far too much rhetoric in this area. Almost every nature programme on television seems to end with such rhetoric. Someone in my profession tends to be particularly allergic to the parsonical voice. Yet you seldom hear it in pulpits today. Instead it seems to have taken residence in nature programmes. 'Just look at these wonderful animals, these magnificent birds or this amazing wilderness ... human beings are on the point of destroying it.' Sermons breathing hell-fire are difficult to find in churches, but their secular counterparts can be heard almost every day on the box. Alternatively, there is positive rhetoric, lacking in self-criticism. The amount of New Age literature easily exceeds conventional religious literature in many bookshops (in Canterbury as elsewhere), and much of it seems to me as a theologian to be astonishingly precritical. Having spent a whole academic career subjecting my own religious faith to every kind of critical perspective and hermeneutic, I find this seriously lacking in much of the New Age literature which I have read. One hundred and fifty years of critical theological scholarship is simply bypassed.

I will try to explore some of the critical questions, both negative and positive, involved in links between religion and the environment, starting with the negative and finishing with the positive. In the process, I hope to uncover some of the pitfalls religious faith needs to avoid, as well as some of the opportunities that it may still have, even in a pluralist world, to make an effective contribution to the environmental debate. Perhaps I should also explain that, although I am obviously a

Christian theologian myself, I am convinced that the global nature of the environmental debate raises similar challenges for many different forms of religious faith. More than that, if human beings are to find answers to these challenges, they will need to cooperate across their religious differences.

The Negative Debate

The most discussed negative critique of the relationship between religion and the environment is surely that of the Californian historian Lynn White. In a celebrated article in the journal *Science* in 1967, he argued that Judaism and Christianity have been responsible for fostering a negative and destructive view of the natural environment. In words that have been repeated many times over within the ecological movement, White (himself a churchgoer) concluded:

> Especially in its Western form, Christianity is the most anthropocentric religion the world has seen. As early as the 2nd century both Tertullian and Saint Irenaeus of Lyons were insisting that when God shaped Adam he was foreshadowing the image of the incarnate Christ, the Second Adam. Man shares, in great measure, God's transcendence of nature. Christianity, in absolute contrast to ancient paganism and Asia's religions (except, perhaps, Zoroastrianism), not only established a dualism of man and nature, but also insisted that it is God's will that man exploit nature for his proper ends.[1]

It is easy to dismiss this claim out of hand. White was given to some very sweeping claims about Christianity and its cultural role in giving rise to destructive Western technology. Many other scholars have noted that the swift summaries of whole civilizations made in this relatively brief article are breathtaking.[2] The trouble with such sweeping summaries is that they

---

[1] Lynn White, 'The Historical Roots of our Ecologic Crisis', *Science* 155, no. 3767 (10 March 1967), pp. 1203–7.
[2] See further Michael S. Northcott, *The Environment and Christian Ethics* (Cambridge: Cambridge University Press, 1996), and section four of my *A Textbook of Christian Ethics* (Edinburgh: T&T Clark, 1995).

can so easily be reversed. So it is just as possible to argue that the Judaeo-Christian heritage has given Western culture a unique set of values to question destructive uses of technology, as it is to argue that this heritage created a conducive environment for this technology in the first place. How do you decide between such sweeping options? Even the great sociologist Max Weber came unstuck making fascinating, but finally sweeping and unprovable, generalizations about this heritage (in his case, about the origins of capitalism).

Lynn White was convinced that a notion of 'dominion' over the environment was fundamental to many Jewish and Christian forms of faith. Most famously in Genesis 1.26, 'God said: "Let us make humankind in our image, according to our likeness; and let them have dominion over the fish of the sea, and over the birds of the air, and over the cattle, and over all the wild animals of earth, and over every creeping thing that creeps upon the earth"' (*NRSV*). But, again, it is frequently pointed out that the word 'dominion', notoriously used to translate the Hebrew in this verse, emphatically does not mean what we witnessed in the Transkei . . . or in Southern California for that matter. Some theologians argue that a notion of 'trusteeship' rather than 'dominion' might be more theologically appropriate, especially if we compare the ideas about creation in Genesis 1 with those in Genesis 2. I will return to this notion of 'trusteeship' later.

Nevertheless, despite its hyperbole, Lynn White's article has still been very effective in alerting theologians to some of the unintended consequences of their ideas. Frankly, Genesis 1.26 *has* sometimes been interpreted as 'dominion' in the crudest and most anthropocentric sense. It is worth remembering that Thomas Aquinas, surely one of the greatest theologians in history, is hardly edifying on this point. Teaching generations of theological students, I find that I have to put Aquinas into context if they are to approach his writings here with any kind of sympathy. With the benefit of huge hindsight, his presumptions about women, slaves and the environment are, I am afraid, politically incorrect in the extreme. His argument starts well, but ends miserably. He starts with the belief that God alone 'is the ultimate end of the whole of things; that an intellectual nature alone attains to him in himself'. He then argues that man as the most intellectual and rational of creatures is

nearest to God. At this point, though, his argument deterio-
rates. Woman is less intellectual and rational than man and, on
this account, subordinate. In turn, the slave is subordinate to
the freeman. Finally, the beast, lacking intellect and rationality,
is subordinate to people as a whole. Indeed, the whole function
of the beast is to serve humanity. Aquinas even explains away
those verses in Deuteronomy which seem to forbid cruelty to
animals with the argument that 'a person through practising
cruelty on brutes might go on to do the same to men'.[3]

This is not meant to be a history lesson. The historical
example is intended only as a warning. It *is* all too easy to hold
views which have unnoticed yet destructive consequences. We
look back on our ancestors and wonder aloud 'How could they
hold that?' Just occasionally we stop and remember that future
generations will surely do the same to us. Aquinas, great
intellect though he was, was still a man (emphatically a man) of
his time and particular culture. He simply assumed that slavery
and the greater intellect of men over women were parts of the
fixed natural order. In a less crowded and environmentally
destructive world, he also failed to notice the danger of his
views about non-humans. We respond with indignation and
then remember, perhaps, that our successors are likely to be
just as indignant with us ... indignant, that is, about issues we
have yet to notice. So let us move to the present without
forgetting the warning history implicitly carries. Whether or not
historical Judaism and Christianity are implicated in environmentally destructive attitudes and behaviour, can the same be
said of the religiously active today? There is now a growing
literature of international sociological research assessing
whether or not White's thesis can be corroborated empirically
in present-day society.[4] Overwhelmingly, it has found no

---

[3] Thomas Aquinas, *Summa Contra Gentiles* (London and New York:
University of Notre Dame Press, 1975), 3.2.112–13.
[4] See Andrew Greeley, 'Religion and Attitudes Toward the Environment',
Journal for the Scientific Study of Religion 32:1 (1993); Michael P. Hornsby-Smith
and Michael Procter, 'Catholic Identity, Religious Context and Environmental
Values in Western Europe: Evidence from the European Values Surveys',
Social Compass 42:1 (1995); Douglas Lee Eckberg and T. Jean Blocker,
'Christianity, Environmentalism, and the Theoretical Problem of Funda-
mentalism', *Journal for the Scientific Study of Religion* 35:4 (1996); Alan W. Black,

significant correlation between religious belief or belonging today and environmentally damaging beliefs, attitudes or behaviour.

In my own recent research over the last few years I have been analysing the attitudes and stated behaviour of churchgoers, testing whether or not they are significantly different from those of non-churchgoers, and then relating the findings to the recent debates in Christian ethics. [This research was published in August 1999 in my series for Cambridge University Press with the title *Churchgoing and Christian Ethics*]. As far as I am aware, this sort of systematic empirical research in Christian ethics has never been done before. When I started it, a number of my colleagues looked extremely sceptical. They were not sure where I would find the necessary data and, even if I could, they were convinced that the data would not show much. Alternatively, they warned that the data might show that churchgoers are more sexist, racist, pro-capital punishment and anti-environment than other people. In the event I found that there is a mass of largely unanalysed data in two major sources, *British Social Attitudes* and the *British Household Panel Survey*, which from now on I will refer to as *BSA* and *BHPS* respectively.[5] Together these two sources give a total database of well over 50,000 respondents, who, amongst a host of other questions (sometimes on the environment), are usually asked whether or not they belong to a religious organization or go regularly to worship.

In the course of this research I have tested a whole range of responses to questions about moral attitudes and behaviour. As it happens, churchgoing (I use this term in a generic sense) is a highly significant variable on most moral issues. Perhaps it is not surprising that the views of churchgoers differ significantly from those of occasional churchgoers and non-churchgoers on such issues as sexuality – although, as the 1998 Lambeth Conference showed, churchgoers are not

---

'Religion and Environmentally Protective Behaviour in Australia', *Social Compass* 44:3 (1997); and Paul Dekker, Peter Ester and Masja Nas, 'Religion, Culture and Environmental Concern: An Empirical Cross-national Analysis', *Social Compass* 44:3 (1997).

[5] The data used here were made available through Data Archive. Neither the original collectors of the data nor the Archive bear any responsibility for the analyses or interpretations presented here.

actually united even on this issue (see chapter 3). Profound differences can be found between churchgoers and others on issues of justice, law-keeping, moral order, honesty and altruism. Regular churchgoers are two or three times more likely than non-churchgoers to be involved in secular voluntary service in the community, they are more charitable, more concerned about the poor overseas, less supportive of capital punishment, less racist, and, oddly, far less likely to smoke. In fact it is difficult to find a moral issue where churchgoing is not a statistically significant variable. Sociologists of religion have been curiously neglectful here. Their counterparts in other areas of sociology or social policy would love to find a similar, yet neglected, variable.

But what about the attitudes of churchgoers towards the environment? My research shows that most weekly churchgoers (86 per cent in *BSA* 1993) agree that, 'human beings should respect nature because it was created by God'. Sometimes it is forgotten in this debate that belief in a creator God might actually enhance rather than diminish respect for the environment. Secondly, my research (in both *BSA* and *BHPS*) shows that churchgoers are more likely than non-churchgoers to be members of an environmental group. For example, in *BHPS* 1991 some 13 per cent of the whole sample claimed membership of a religious group, but amongst those who were members of an environmental group this rose to 21 per cent. Again, whereas 18 per cent of the whole sample claimed to go to church at least once a month, this rose to 30 per cent in the environmental group. Of course most environmentalists are not regular churchgoers, nor do they belong to a religious group. It would be foolish to claim that *formal* religious belonging is a central feature of life for most environmentalists. Such a claim is certainly not necessary for my argument here. It is sufficient to show that environmentalists do seem to be more involved in churches and other religious organizations than the population at large.

Other questions in *BSA* 1994 suggest that churchgoers are also more likely than other people to act on environmental issues. In one scenario it was suggested that 'a housing development was being planned in a part of the countryside you knew and liked' and respondents were asked what if anything they might do about this. Churchgoers differed from non-churchgoers in that they said that they would contact their MP or councillor (47 per cent of weekly churchgoers; 41 per cent of monthly churchgoers; 37 per cent of occasional church-goers; 29 per cent those who seldom or never go; and 29 per cent of those who say they have 'no religion') and contact a government or planning department (the figures this time, 21 per cent; 11 per cent; 20 per cent; 12 per cent; and 12 per cent respectively).

In a second scenario, it was suggested that 'a site where wildflowers grew was going to be ploughed for farmland'. On this, too, churchgoers appeared different in that they 'would take action' (15 per cent; 5 per cent; 8 per cent; 9 per cent; compared to 4 per cent of those with no religion). Asked more bluntly about what they had actually done 'to help to protect the countryside', more churchgoers than non-churchgoers said that they had contacted their MP or councillor (16 per cent; 7 per cent; 10 per cent; 6 per cent; compared to 6 per cent). Once again, these patterns suggest that churchgoers in modern Britain are not especially apathetic about, let alone hostile to, environmental issues. If anything, the reverse seems to be the case.

Obviously there are many churchgoers here who show little awareness of environmental issues. These issues did, however, reach the agenda at the recent Lambeth Conference, and the environment sub-section produced a very creditable report, but environmentalism still did not figure prominently in the plenary debates. Speaking personally, I wish that even a quarter of the time and energy given to the issue of homosexuality at the Conference had been given to environmental issues. Perhaps at the next Conference we can expect more. Yet, for the moment, there are signs that churchgoers are not lacking in environmental sensitivity. I believe that there are some very positive, theological reasons why this should indeed be the case.

The Positive Debate

It is time to turn to the positive side of the debate. Does religious faith have something distinctive and powerful to contribute to the environmental debate? I believe that it does. If the Lynn White article has forced theologians to look more deeply at some of our negative roots, perhaps it has also encouraged us to identify some of the positive ones as well. It may also have encouraged theologians to look more critically at some of the secular arguments that have been used in the environmental debate. Having dismissed the Judaeo-Christian heritage as environmentally damaging, some secularists have assumed that this heritage has nothing further of any use to contribute. Perhaps they have never read to the end of Lynn White's original article. As an active, yet critical, Christian himself, he argued that there are some versions of Christianity which are environmentally friendly. He was particularly attracted to the Franciscans. Here, at least, was a community of Christians with a rich tradition of respect for the natural world, for God's world. Lynn White's own theological ideas are largely undeveloped. Yet they do seem to be implicit in his position.

There are three key beliefs held by people of many different religious traditions. For people of religious faith they are both interconnected and distinct from purely secular outlooks. The first of these is that life, both human and non-human, is created and God-given; the second is that creation is purposeful; and the third is that human beings have a sacred duty towards God's creation. Now, of course, there are secular counterparts to each of these beliefs. Many secularists hold that life, especially human life, is special and uniquely valuable, that life if it is treated as valuable can properly be endowed with purpose, and that valuing life should encourage us to care for both all things living and the environment in which they live. After all, they often argue, this is the only world that we have, so we had better take care of it. I certainly do not wish to belittle this secular vision in any way. I have never been able to understand why religious people should attack every secular vision even when it serves similar ends to their own. However, I believe that a theistic vision offers a different and more powerful level of conviction. It argues that it is not simply a question of human beings choosing to value life but rather being convinced that life is already valued by God who created it. Or, to express this technically, it is a conviction based upon ontology and not simply upon volition.

Let me take each of these three religious beliefs in turn. They need to be expressed carefully.

The first holds that life, both human and non-human, is created and God-given. Of course within different religious traditions there are various ways of expressing this belief. Jews, Christians and Muslims all use the language of 'creation' and 'God-givenness'. Monistic religious traditions will probably prefer to talk about life as 'sacred'. Even those versions of Buddhism which explicitly reject any belief in God still hold a deeply religious understanding of life. Many different forms of religious tradition, Eastern and Western, are united in believing that religious faith endows life, especially human life, with a transcendent meaning. All offer a sharp contrast to purely secular materialists.

However, this is a belief that increasingly divides the British. In theory, two-thirds of the population still expresses some belief in God while, at the most, one in four claims to be an atheist. Yet the way theistic belief is expressed, especially in the environmental debate, does divide us. *BSA* 1993 offered people a choice between three claims: 'nature is sacred because it is created by God'; 'nature is spiritual or sacred in itself'; and 'nature is important, but not spiritual or sacred'. These three responses might be labelled as the theistic, monistic and secular respectively. Respondents were asked to choose just one of these three options. Majority support for the first option, the theistic option, is found only amongst weekly churchgoers (54 per cent), and has little support amongst non-churchgoers (16 per cent) and the no-religion group (8 per cent). Majority support for the third option, the secular option, is found especially in the no-religion group (66 per cent) and shows clear and statistically significant differences between church-goers and non-churchgoers (35 per cent weekly churchgoers; 39 per cent monthly churchgoers; 57 per cent occasional churchgoers; and 59 per cent those who seldom or never go to church). The middle option, the monistic option, is a minority choice in all groups. It has highest support amongst the no-religion group and, for some reason, amongst monthly churchgoers. Yet, even then this support only amounts to 16 per cent. Amongst weekly churchgoers it reduces to just 4 per cent. So, in theory, three distinct groups – regular churchgoers, non-churchgoers and the no-religion group – agree that nature is to be taken seriously. In the sample as a whole, only 19 per cent actually *disagreed* with the claim, 'human beings should

respect nature because it was created by God'. Yet, when given
a choice of these three options, 'God language' is clearly more
attractive to regular churchgoers, and secularized, or alternatively 'new age', language to the no-religion group, with
non-churchgoers responding more ambivalently.

Yet, especially for religious Jews, Christians and Muslims, a
doctrine of creation has very powerful implications for how we
should treat the world around us. The Jewish Bible, for
example, is saturated with the idea that the promised land is
God-given and, on this account, deserves particular respect. As
a gift it should be received gratefully and responsibly. Just to
give a single example from Deuteronomy:

> [T]he Lord your God is bringing you to a rich land, a land of
> streams, of springs and underground waters gushing out in
> hill and valley, a land of wheat and barley, of vines, fig-trees,
> and pomegranates, a land of olives, oil, and honey. It is a land
> where you will never live in poverty nor want for anything, a
> land whose stones are iron-ore and from whose hills you will
> dig copper. You will have plenty to eat and will bless the Lord
> your God for the rich land that he has given you.[6]

Now of course this vision from Deuteronomy can be idealized.
Deuteronomy itself contains many unwitting reminders that the
Israelites were in the process of dispossessing other people —
the Canaanites, the Jebuzites, and so forth — of *their* God-given
land. Even the language of 'gift' can be distorted. Surely it is no
accident that in German the word *gift* simply means poison.
Gifts, even God's gifts, can be distorted and God's gifts to other
people can be trampled upon. Yet the primary intention of
Deuteronomy is surely to remind readers that this beautiful
land, this Holy Land, does not finally belong to people. It
belongs properly to God.

Perhaps this point can be captured using another metaphor,
that of 'trusteeship'. Land is entrusted to the people of Israel but
belongs properly to God and not to them. It is entrusted to the
present generation for the sake of generations to come. Land is
to be preserved unharmed for the sake of life yet unborn ... for
generations upon generations upon generations. That is exactly

---

[6] Deut. 8.7–10 (*NEB*).

what a charitable trust is. Until recently it was fashionable in environmental theology to use the metaphor of 'stewardship'. Using this metaphor, we are required not to have 'dominion' over God's land but to be careful stewards of it. However, the philosopher Stephen R.L. Clark notes sarcastically, in his splendid book *How to Think About the Earth*, that 'better be a steward, maybe, than a simple pirate – but what else did pirates ever do when they grew tired of travel or the travel-ships were few? ... to secure their status, and prevent the outbreak of rash sentiment among the young, they claimed to be God's messengers, and built pyramids'.[7] Stewards still manage and change things for their own benefit. Trustees are required to be concerned about others and, indeed, about the future.

The second belief that is held in many religious traditions follows naturally. It is that creation is purposeful. The universe is not arbitrary or fortuitous ... it has a 'telos', a purpose or meaningful end. For Jews, Christians and Muslims, God created the universe in love and brought order to what would otherwise be chaos. All things are finally directed to God as creator. In God they are created, sustained and finally completed. In God they receive purpose and meaning. Monotheistic faith, especially, is irresistibly teleological.

Some see this as the key point of warfare between science and religion. Thomas Huxley in the nineteenth century and Richard Dawkins today are good examples.[8] On the one hand, they tend to claim, there is the rational world of science which accepts that the universe can have no meaning or purpose. On the other, is the out-moded world of religion which insists that it can. True scientists know that Darwin made any language of purpose within the natural world superfluous and unnecessary. The genius of Darwin was to show that human life could evolve slowly through a series of random changes which favoured some forms of life rather than others. Arbitrary change rather

---

[7] Stephen R.L. Clark, *How to Think About the Earth: Philosophical and Theological Models for Ecology* (London: Mowbray, 1993), p. 108.

[8] For a sustained critique of Dawkins see Stephen R.L. Clark's *Biology and Christian Ethics* (Cambridge: Cambridge University Press, 2000) and also David Martin (chapter 10 below). For a seminal account of the nineteenth-century debates about science and religion, see John Hedley Brooke's *Science and Religion* (Cambridge: Cambridge University Press, 1991).

than purposeful order finally characterizes the environment and everything in it.

I have expressed this clash of culture crudely because that is how it is sometimes presented, even in the university world. In reality, Charles Darwin had theological supporters and scientific critics from the outset. The theologian Frederick Temple was an early and outspoken supporter of evolution, arguing with others that it actually helped us to understand better how (but not why) God created the universe. Of course some theologians at the time, and neo-conservatives today, saw Darwin's theories as inherently opposed to religious faith. As early as 1860, Temple argued otherwise. Amazingly, by 1897 he had been appointed Archbishop of Canterbury. It is odd that this particular battle is still fought today.

A conviction that the universe really does have an underlying purpose is important for the environmental debate. The person who has this conviction is given an even stronger reason for believing that parts of this amazing universe are not to be wilfully destroyed. It should make us hesitant about radically changing the natural order, about 'playing God' if you like. I do not believe this means that we should simply abandon biotechnology, which offers a genuine prospect of cures from egregious genetic conditions and of improved food to feed a hungry world. However, it does mean that we are right to encourage our scientists to act prudently and responsibly. The powers that physics and now genetics have unleashed in the twentieth century have raised crucial ethical issues and have reminded us, as never before, that power is seldom neutral. It can be used for the good of human beings *and* their environment, or sadly it can be used for their destruction.

Thank God so many scientists today are aware of this. If once it might have been argued that science and technology are morally neutral, today we hear this claim less often. Yet once people are aware of this, an obvious problem arises. How are we to make ethical judgements? In medical ethics – the area of science where these issues have been most debated – a clash is increasingly evident. For some, free choice and informed consent are *the* guiding principles of medical ethics. I agree that they are important and have no wish to return to more paternalistic forms of medicine in which patients were often given no choice, let alone adequate information on which to make a proper choice. Yet for many of us, justice and beneficence (literally doing good) are also key principles of medical ethics. From a perspective of religious faith, they are surely vital. In a world created purposefully, there are always broader issues beyond the individual to be considered.

This leads to the third religious belief, namely that human beings have a sacred duty towards God's creation. Once convinced that life is already valued by God who created it, we have every reason to believe that we, in turn, have a duty towards this creation. In my research on churchgoing I found that altruism – a concern for others – is a highly significant feature of regular churchgoers. I have already mentioned the high involvement of churchgoers in voluntary service in the community. Even apparently secular charities such as Oxfam find that many of their volunteers are churchgoers. In addition, churchgoers are twice as likely as other people to say that 'helping others' is the most important factor in choosing a new job, or that charitable money should be given to starving people overseas. Conversely, churchgoers are much less likely than others to believe that 'we should support more charities which benefit people in Britain, rather than people overseas'. The proverb that 'charity begins at home' belongs more to non-churchgoers than to churchgoers.

Once again, these data can be exaggerated. Real differences in attitude and behaviour can be measured between churchgoers and others in modern Britain, but they are relative not absolute differences. It will hardly surprise you that not all churchgoers are altruistic. And, of course, many people who say they have no religion at all are altruistic. A concern for other people is certainly not a monopoly of churchgoers. It is not a monopoly, but it does appear to be more common amongst churchgoers.

A concern for others is also a feature of many different religious traditions. In his recent book *A Global Ethic as a Foundation for Global Society*,[9] Hans Küng identifies a 'golden rule of humanity' which can be found across many faiths. He cites the following:

[9] London: SCM Press, 1997, pp. 98–9

Confucius: 'What you yourself do not want, do not do to another person.'

Rabbi Hillel: 'Do not do to others what you would not want them to do to you.'

Jesus: 'Whatever you want people to do to you, do also to them.'

Islam: 'None of you is a believer as long as he does not wish his brother what he wishes himself.'

Jainism: 'Human beings should be indifferent to worldly things and treat all creatures in the world as they would want to be treated themselves.'

Buddhism: 'A state which is not pleasant or enjoyable for me will also not be so for him; and how can I impose on another a state which is not pleasant or enjoyable for me?'

Hinduism: 'One should not behave towards others in a way which is unpleasant for oneself: that is the essence of morality.'

An important feature of Hans Küng's argument is that global issues, such as the environment, do require human beings to be altruistic – that is, to act beyond self-interest – across their religious traditions and different cultures. He is well aware that Christians have distinctive theological reasons for acting beyond self-interest. Not the least of our reasons is that we believe that on the cross Jesus Christ gave his life for us and for our salvation. Christians do not need to renounce this fundamental belief to be convinced that different religious traditions can and should build upon their shared heritage of altruism. This heritage now needs to encompass not just the human stranger but the non-human as well.

Taken as a whole, the three religious beliefs that I have outlined offer a sharp contrast to any secular creed based only upon narrow self-interest. If we are to address the huge issues of the environment confronting us today, then somehow we do have to move beyond self-interest. Tackling human over-population and over-consumption, which have resulted in such appalling pollution, soil erosion, deforestation and species extinction, requires us to make an immense moral change. I believe that religious traditions do have the inner resources necessary for such a change. In short, as I said at the outset, the environmental debate is as much about religion and morality as it is about science.

2

The Arms Trade

If the environment represents one of the key moral issues of our age, I believe that the globalization of the arms trade represents another. And yet, compared with the environment, the arms trade has not received sufficient attention from Christian ethicists. Perhaps it is the daunting complexity of the arms trade – a complexity that is unlikely to be penetrated by those of us who instinctively despise it. Or perhaps it is the secrecy that surrounds national arms possessions and patterns of trading and transfer, a secrecy shored up by legitimate concerns about national security as well as by more dubious vested economic and political interests. Whatever the reasons, the terrifying escalation of the arms trade around the world does require very careful moral and theological attention. If ever there was an area in need of change, it is surely this, especially after the shock the world has had in the devastation of September 11 and subsequent events.

In this chapter I will focus upon the arms trade (or, more accurately, upon international if not global arms transfer), albeit set in the specific context of the recent wars or conflicts in the 1990s, first in the Gulf, then in Iraq and finally in the Balkans, and in the wars against global terrorism that are emerging in the new millennium.

An obvious place to start is with Christian versions of just-war theory. Although initially derived by Ambrose and Augustine from pre-Christian, Greek and Roman sources, just-war theory has long been shaped by Christian theologians and now represents one of the more abiding theological heirlooms in the modern world.[1] It is intentionally a limiting framework. Given that countries are, and always have been, tempted on occasions

---

[1] See further my *A Textbook of Christian Ethics* (Edinburgh: T&T Clark, 1995), section 3.

to go to war, just-war theory introduces notes of moral caution
into a situation. It offers broad criteria in order to encourage
people to see some forms of warfare as considerably less justified
than others. Down the centuries, many Christians have voiced
strong anxieties about warfare and have sought to constrain
countries from going lightly into battle and then to limit the
horrors of war once it starts.

The highly influential 1983 pastoral letter of the United
States Catholic Bishops, *The Challenge of Peace*, illustrates this
point well. Early in this letter, they explain the concept of
comparative justice, which they believe is essential for a proper
understanding of just-war theory, as follows:

> Questions concerning the *means* of waging war today, particu-
> larly in view of the destructive potential of weapons, have
> tended to override questions concerning the comparative
> justice of the positions of respective adversaries or enemies. In
> essence: which side is sufficiently 'right' in a dispute, and are
> the values at stake critical enough to override the presumption
> against war? The question in its most basic form is this: do
> the rights and values involved justify killing? For whatever the
> means used, war, by definition, involves violence, destruction,
> suffering, and death. The category of comparative justice is
> designed to emphasize the presumption against war which
> stands at the beginning of just-war teaching. In a world of
> sovereign states recognizing neither a common moral
> authority nor a central political authority, comparative justice
> stresses that no state should act on the basis that it has
> 'absolute justice' on its side. Every party to a conflict should
> acknowledge the limits of its 'just cause' and the consequent
> requirement to use only limited means in pursuit of its objec-
> tives. Far from legitimizing a crusade mentality, comparative
> justice is designed to relativize absolute claims and to restrain
> the use of force even in a 'justified' conflict. Given techniques
> of propaganda and the ease with which nations and
> individuals either assume or delude themselves into believing
> that God or right is clearly on their side, the test of
> comparative justice may be extremely difficult to apply.[2]

[2] United States Catholic Bishops, *The Challenge of Peace: God's Promise and Our
Response* (National Conference of Catholic Bishops, Washington DC and
CTS/SPCK, 3 May 1983), paras 92–4.

The clear logic of this is that just-war theory, especially in the modern world, is intended primarily to be a constraint upon war rather than a means of justifying particular wars.

Within just-war theory, different principles are important actually within a war (*ius in bello*) from those before a war (*ius ad bellum*). In both cases, just-war theory seeks to limit damage, but does so rather differently. Within a war (whether or not it was considered to be justified in the first place) the principles of discrimination and proportionality receive particular attention. It is claimed that the increasing sophistication of modern weapons has allowed rockets and bombs to be deployed in conflict with a much greater capacity for target discrimination than hitherto and that modern weapons can usually discriminate between military and civilian targets. The bombings by the United Nations in the Gulf, by NATO in the Balkans and then by the Americans in Afghanistan have, of course, raised many doubts about this claim: according to some estimates a tenth of bombs and missiles dropped are likely not to explode, leaving a legacy of unexploded weapons, and at least a tenth miss their military targets altogether. Both outcomes inevitably result in civilian casualties. A concern of Western countries to be seen to act in accordance with international agreements – either those of the United Nations or those of NATO – has entailed a new carefulness in deploying proportionate military resources, and the effects of media reporting upon home and enemy populations have also encouraged a more fastidious approach to both discrimination and proportionality within military engagements.

A complex mixture of increasing public awareness, digitized weapons and post-cold-war political alliances has put a new (and welcome) emphasis upon these two ethical principles which have historically attempted to limit the evil effects that occur within the context of warfare (*ius in bello*). Indeed, the principles of discrimination and proportionality were widely discussed in the sophisticated media at the very outset of the war against al-Qaeda in Afghanistan.

However, a broader set of principles has been developed over the centuries to test the morality of going to war at all (*ius ad bellum*). Most modern forms of just-war theory contain at least the following additional elements. For a war to be considered 'just', it must:

1) have been undertaken by a lawful authority;
2) have been undertaken for the vindication of an undoubted right that has certainly been infringed;
3) be a last resort, all peaceful means of settlement having
   failed;
4) offer the possibility of the good achieved outweighing the
   evils that war would involve;
5) be waged with right intention;
6) be waged with a reasonable hope of victory for justice.

Disputes about the moral legitimacy of the Gulf, Iraq, Balkan
and Afghanistan wars have focused upon the first, third and
sixth criteria. For many commentators, the Gulf war satisfied
the first criterion most clearly since it was authorized by the
United Nations and was halted when the United Nations'
mandate expired. In contrast, the Iraq and Afghanistan
bombings were, arguably, legitimated at the outset only by the
United States and Britain (although President Bush and Prime
Minister Blair did go to considerable lengths to form as wide an
alliance as possible in the weeks before bombing Afghanistan).
The Balkans bombing, legitimated by NATO rather than by the
United Nations, appeared to be halfway between these
positions. Whether NATO, designed as a defensive alliance
against a presumed Soviet enemy, had the authority to
intervene remains disputed.

The third criterion appeared to many to fit the Gulf war
most clearly, since many nations considered at the outset that
a clear and dangerous act of aggression had already taken
place, thus precluding peaceful means of settlement (and also
satisfying the second criterion). In the 1999 Balkan war, the
Russian government clearly believed that NATO countries had
not exhausted all peaceful negotiations, although critics were
not convinced that it, in turn, had exhausted peaceful means
before bombarding Grozny in Chechnya later in the same
year. This was also a point of considerable dispute in the
earlier Falklands war. Did the British government really
exhaust all peaceful means in what many other nations
regarded as a long-standing, ambiguous territorial dispute
before engaging in the war? And, in particular, did Mrs
Thatcher go through all the peaceful options before ordering
the *Belgrano* to be sunk?

Prophetically, the US Catholic Bishops recognized just how contentious these two criteria were likely to become in the modern world:

> For resort to war to be justified, all peaceful alternatives must have been exhausted. There are formidable problems in this requirement. No international organization currently in existence has exercised sufficient internationally recognized authority to be able either to mediate effectively in most cases or to prevent conflict by the intervention of United Nations or other peacekeeping forces. Furthermore, there is a tendency for nations or peoples which perceive conflict between or among other nations as advantageous to themselves to attempt to prevent a peaceful settlement rather than advance it. We regret the apparent unwillingness of some to see in the United Nations organization the potential for world order which exists and to encourage its development. Pope Paul VI called the United Nations the last hope for peace. The loss of this hope cannot be allowed to happen.[3]

In the aftermath of the Gulf war it was hoped that the United Nations really would be able to have a crucial role in constraining and policing warfare in the modern world. Unfortunately the Iraq and Balkan wars considerably undermined this hope and at the outset of the war against al-Qaeda in Afghanistan the role of the United Nations was remarkably *sotto voce.*

However, it is the sixth criterion and, in part, the fourth which have proved the most troublesome in all recent wars. The Gulf war may have stopped Iraq's conquest of Kuwait, but it manifestly did not stop Iraqi aggression. Neither the bombing of Iraq nor the 1999 bombing in the Balkans achieved any complete 'victory for justice', but, instead, rather helped to foster the deep anti-American sentiments of al-Qaeda and its supporters in the Muslim world. Even the surrender of the Serbs following the NATO bombing produced at best an ambiguous 'victory for justice'. Indeed, some would argue that the evils of modern warfare make the achievement of either the fourth or sixth criterion unlikely.

[3] *The Challenge of Peace,* paras 96–7.

On this understanding, the full array of modern weapons (which still includes nuclear weapons) has become just too dangerous to be used any more as a means of achieving even the vindication of an undoubted right that has certainly been infringed.

This final point raises perhaps the most difficult issue of all. Even if modern warfare can be fought with a remarkable degree of discrimination and proportionality, is it finally a moral way of 'policing' the world? Those who believe this is so, often use the analogy of a police force. In a fallen world, nations as well as people do need to be restrained and deterred at times from doing evil. The international community does properly act on occasions as a sort of police force to protect the vulnerable – whether they are the people of Kuwait, Kosovo or New York.

But there are still problems. Supposing the Soviet Union had won the Cold War, would British Christians be quite so keen to see them rather than Americans acting as the police force of the world? We cannot be so confident that military superiority in the future will remain firmly in the hands of friendly democracies. There have, after all, been many examples of tyrannical, undemocratic countries using their superior military power to 'police' weaker countries. Unless we find effective, non-military means of resolving all national, international and global conflicts, our long-term future may be bleak. In other words, just-war theory in the future may need to insist that peaceful means of settlement must not be allowed to fail.

What implications does all of this have for the international arms trade? Weapons of mass destruction should cause us considerable anxiety and it is, I believe, right that we should seek to constrain their proliferation and, especially, their use. In his important 1992 report *Profit Without Honour? Ethics and the Arms Trade* for the Council on Christian Approaches to Defence and Disarmament, Roger Williamson argues that there is a broad consensus emerging across different churches. Having reviewed a rich variety of church statements and reports produced during the last three decades, he concludes:

> The accumulated evidence of the church statements of the British churches, European churches, the Roman Catholic Church (both centrally and in its national episcopal

conferences), as well as international ecumenical bodies presents an increasingly clear voice in favour of bringing the arms trade under stricter control based upon moral principles. There are persistent pleas for greater openness and an insistence that the arms industry should not be allowed to be so dominant that pressure to sell arms overrides ethical considerations.[4]

If this trade is indeed to be brought under 'stricter control based upon moral principles', then applying just-war theory rigorously – in terms of the criteria for use within war and those for use in advance of war – is an obvious way to do this. If this could be achieved, then the hope would be that just-war theory might be able to constrain both the proliferation and use of weapons of war.

The principles of discrimination and proportionality have important implications for the arms trade. Once again the US Catholic Bishops recognized this clearly in their pastoral letter:

> In terms of the arms race, if the real end in view is legitimate defence against unjust aggression, and the means to this end are not evil in themselves, we must still examine the question of proportionality concerning attendant evils. Do the exorbitant costs, the general climate of insecurity generated, the possibility of accidental detonation of highly destructive weapons, the danger of error and miscalculation that could provoke retaliation and war – do such evils or others attendant upon and indirectly deriving from the arms race make the arms race itself a disproportionate response to aggression? Pope John Paul II is very clear in his insistence that the exercise of the right and duty of a people to protect their existence and freedom is contingent on the use of proportionate means.[5]

In contrast, those who support indiscriminate trade typically do so on the basis of a number of supposedly value-neutral or consequential grounds. So they might argue that it is not the

---

[4] Roger Williamson, *Profit Without Honour? Ethics and the Arms Trade* (The Council on Christian Approaches to Defence and Disarmament, St Bride Foundation Institute, Bride Lane, London EC4Y 8EQ, and Methodist Publishing House, 20 Ivatt Way, Peterborough, PE3 7PQ), pp. 106–7.
[5] US Catholic Bishops, *The Challenge of Peace*, para. 107.

buying or selling, or even transferring, of arms that is morally objectionable but their use. Arms are a form of technology and, like all forms of technology, they can be used properly or improperly. It is the people who own arms who are the moral (or immoral) agents, not the arms themselves.

A more sophisticated version of this argument would maintain that if it is legitimate for any particular nation to possess certain types of weapons, for whatever reasons, then it cannot be wrong for any other nation to possess them as well for the same reasons. So, if it is considered right that one nation should have a set of weapons with which to defend itself, then it must be right that other nations should be allowed to defend themselves similarly. Of course this might change if you suspect that some nations wish to have such weapons for aggressive rather than purely defensive purposes. However, it is not wrong in itself to possess weapons which can be used for defensive purposes. Possession as such is morally neutral.

Unfortunately there is an obvious flaw in this argument. It could be used successfully to defend horizontal nuclear proliferation. (In this context, horizontal nuclear proliferation involves the spread of nuclear weapons into more and more countries, whereas vertical nuclear proliferation involves the production of ever more powerful nuclear weapons.) Presumably those countries possessing nuclear weapons believe that they remain important for the maintenance of peace within the world. During the Cold War, carefully articulated policies of nuclear deterrence depended upon such notions as a balance of nuclear weapons between the superpowers and threatened mutual assured destruction. Even though there is now considerable scepticism about the viability of these policies, a vast number of nuclear weapons do still exist and the number of countries possessing them is still increasing. Presumably nations wish to become nuclear powers precisely because they believe that they will be better able to defend themselves from other nuclear powers with such weapons. Yet this is the Achilles heel of any policy of nuclear deterrence. If possessing nuclear weapons deters others from using them, then everyone should possess them and then no nation will use them. But if everyone possesses them then surely it becomes more, not less, likely that someone, somewhere, sometime may indeed use them.

The US Bishops reached the same conclusion:

We fear that our world and nation are headed in the wrong direction. More weapons with greater destructive potential are produced every day. More and more nations are seeking to become nuclear powers. In our quest for more and more security, we fear we are actually becoming less and less secure.[6]

Jonathan Schell's remarkable 1998 book *The Gift of Time: The Case for Abolishing Nuclear Weapons Now* takes this argument further. He interviewed a wide variety of retired politicians and military, together with a number of leading academics, many of whom were once supporters of nuclear deterrence, but who now recognize it to be a deeply flawed doctrine. The observations of Robert McNamara, one of the architects of the policies of the Kennedy and Johnson administrations in the Vietnam War, are particularly striking. Once thoroughly convinced of the policy of mutual assured destruction, he now argues:

I think it's not only desirable but essential that we eliminate nuclear weapons. They have no military utility other than to deter one's opponents from using nuclear weapons. And if our opponent doesn't have nuclear weapons, we don't need them. I am quoting almost exactly from a National Academy of Sciences report.[7]

There is an obvious difficulty in maintaining such a position even after the end of the Cold War (and even more so after September 11) and McNamara recognizes this immediately:

Now that report, oddly enough having made such a clear-cut and, I think, correct statement, goes on to say that we can't – we shouldn't – go below fifteen hundred or two thousand warheads. The reason they say it's not possible to get rid of nuclear weapons altogether is that we must protect against rogue-state or terrorist breakout.[8]

[6] US Catholic Bishops, *The Challenge of Peace*, para. 332.
[7] Jonathan Schell, *The Gift of Time: The Case for Abolishing Nuclear Weapons Now* (London: Granta Publications, 1998), p. 46.
[8] Schell, *The Gift of Time*, p. 46.

His response to this argument shows just how far his own position has now changed:

> Two or three reasons. The first is that it's very, very risky. Even a low probability of catastrophe is a high risk, and I don't think we should continue to accept it. If you don't believe it's a risk, then read the reports of the Cuban Missile Crisis Retrospective Meetings and the recently published Kennedy tapes. I believe that was the best-managed Cold War crisis of any, but we came within a hairbreadth of nuclear war without realising it. There were mistakes made by Krushchev and his associates, and by Kennedy and his associates, including me ... It's no credit to us that we missed nuclear war ... So I want to say that's a risk I don't believe the human race should accept ... [In addition] using nuclear weapons against a nuclear-equipped opponent of any size at all is suicide, and ... using them against a non-nuclear-equipped opponent is, I think, immoral.[9]

There are also a number of considerably less honourable arguments that are used in defence of an indiscriminate arms trade. The most popular of these is that this is indeed trade which creates employment in Britain and which will simply be undertaken elsewhere in the world if the British do not do it. This is sometimes dubbed the 'slavery argument' since it was deployed by supporters of the slave trade in the eighteenth century. Undoubtedly there is considerable employment generated in Britain by the international arms trade (as there was once by the slave trade). Yet it is not a difficult argument to counter on more principled grounds. Doubtless child prostitution is popular and generates income in some parts of the world, yet few in Britain would seek to introduce it here on these grounds. Just because something is done by others elsewhere and generates employment for them does not make it right that we should do it ourselves. Indeed, within the slavery debate the very opposite conclusions were eventually drawn. The British government decided not just to ban it within Britain but to seek to abolish it elsewhere in the world as well. In the end it was decided that there was no such thing as a just slave trade.

[9] Schell, *The Gift of Time*, pp. 47–8.

Thoroughgoing Christian pacifists are most likely to agree wholeheartedly with this slavery argument. Since they believe that warfare is never justified, they will probably conclude that any trade/transfer in the weapons of warfare is also, like the trade in slaves, itself never justified. The response of just-war Christians is likely to be more complex. Some might argue against purely commercial arms trade, but nonetheless support carefully negotiated defensive arms transfers between those democratic governments that scrupulously uphold human rights. Others might argue that there is a proper place for commerce here but that it must be carefully subordinated to strict ethical criteria. Nonetheless, all of these groups would agree that an indiscriminate arms trade or transfer is wrong, however much employment it generates.

If an indiscriminate arms trade is not to be defended as a just-arms trade, what about the principle of proportionality? There does seem to be a *prima facie* case for arguing that there are weapons of such monstrous proportions, such as nuclear weapons, that they should not be included in any notion of a just arms trade. Yet the trouble here, as the world has suddenly realized following September 11, is that so-called conventional, let alone chemical and biological, weapons are also becoming potentially almost as destructive. The horror at witnessing two civilian airliners being used as weapons of mass destruction awakened everyone to the very serious danger that we all face. Indeed, leading politicians started to talk openly about the possibility of terrorists destroying nuclear power stations near conurbations or finding some means of 'effectively' delivering chemical or biological weapons – quite apart from deploying portable nuclear weapons in city centres. The vertical proliferation of nuclear weapons is increasingly matched by the vertical proliferation of other forms of weapons as well. As William Schweiker analysed so accurately, the central problem is that human beings have become ever more powerful but have failed to develop corresponding corporate practices of social responsibility.[10] Indeed, the combination in the modern world

---

[10] William Schweiker, *Responsibility and Christian Ethics* (Cambridge: Cambridge University Press, 1995).

of vastly enhanced power with increasing moral confusion is potentially disastrous.

Perhaps a distinction might be made between those defensive weapons that can actually be used for purely defensive purposes and those that certainly should not be used for such purposes. It is not difficult to see that there is a difference in kind and not simply in degree between, say, a nuclear bomb and a police truncheon. Both are types of arms and could in theory be bought and sold. Yet a police truncheon is unlikely to kill people if used and has a clear and limited purpose to restrain violent criminals, whereas a nuclear bomb certainly will kill people if detonated in a populated area and will continue to contaminate that area for many years to come. In the hands of a tyrant, a police truncheon will be of little use for aggressive rather than defensive purposes. In contrast, there is a very real fear that a terrorist group or a fanatical tyrant may one day be able to purchase nuclear-grade material and use it to commit an act of atrocity against a civilian population (just as they have already used chemical and biological weapons). As a result of this fear, most people would regard trade involving nuclear weapons as distinctly more questionable than trade involving truncheons.

To return to Jonathan Schell's *The Gift of Time*, he finally argues for a policy of total abolition of nuclear weapons, believing that they have no justifiable use in the world today. He believes that both vertical and horizontal nuclear disarmament are now required:

> If vertical disarmament involves lowering the number of weapons in nuclear arsenals, horizontal disarmament involves progressively standing down, dispersing, disassembling, or partially dismantling arsenals. Establishing ceilings on nuclear arsenals, abolishing certain classes of weapons and drawing down the number of weapons are steps along the vertical path. 'De-alerting' nuclear weapons, 'de-mating' warheads from delivery vehicles, storing warheads at a distance from delivery vehicles, removing parts from warheads or delivery vehicles (or adding parts that spoil their performance), or adulterating weapons-grade fissile materials are steps along the horizontal path. Vertical disarmament makes a catastrophe, should it ever occur, smaller. Horizontal disarmament makes a catastrophe of any size less

likely to occur. The verticalist looks at the size of the arsenals. The horizontalist looks at their operation.[11]

Schell is aware that nuclear weapons cannot strictly be 'dis-invented'. Nuclear knowledge, in both civil and military forms, remains an inescapable part of our world. Yet that does not mean that we have to continue to possess, let alone trade in, nuclear weapons. Even the threat of terrorist groups using nuclear weapons is not, he believes, an argument for govern-ments themselves retaining a residuum of nuclear weapons. Any advantage such groups gained in an otherwise nuclear-free world would at most be very temporary and the very elimination of government weapons would make it less likely than at present that these groups would gain access to them. Exactly the same argument can also be used of chemical and biological weapons. The very fact that governments around the world have secretly continued to develop such weapons has made it more rather than less likely that terrorists will use (and have used) them.

Of course my contrast between nuclear weapons and truncheons is too easy. It becomes very much more difficult to distinguish between defensive and potentially aggressive weapons among those weapons that lie between these two extremes. It must be for others with much more technical expertise than myself to give advice here. Yet it does seem to be a requirement of just-war theory that some such distinction is made. In terms of the criteria appropriate before war is undertaken, the second criterion assumes that just war is always a defensive response and not an initiating act of aggression. In addition, the fifth criterion does insist upon knowing something about the intentions of the one contemplating war. An ethical approach to the arms trade would surely wish to insist upon the same.

The fourth and sixth criteria applied to the arms trade would also forbid selling or transferring weapons to a country in a situation where there was no serious possibility of good outweighing the evils of war or where there was no reasonable hope of victory for justice. If applied rigorously, these two criteria would offend both pragmatists who regard technology

[11] Schell, *The Gift of Time*, pp. 69–70.

itself as value-free and libertarians who consider such judge-ments to be patronizing. However, a principled approach to the arms trade should be concerned about both the buyers and the sellers. If technology is regarded at the outset as potential power and not simply as value-free – power which can be used for good and ill – there is a proper sense of responsibility placed upon those developing and selling or transferring it. And, in contrast to a purely libertarian perspective, there is a strong dimension of social responsibility present in just-war theory. It is for this reason that it insists in the first, and oldest, criterion that private citizens should not be allowed to initiate wars. Only lawful authorities can properly declare war.

It is, though, once again the third criterion that raises serious moral questions. If we conclude that our priority is to find effective, non-military means of resolving all national, inter-national and global conflicts, then the legitimacy of much of the arms trade becomes increasingly questionable. Roger Williamson, arguing from within a Christian just-war position, reaches the same conclusion, but immediately offers a warning:

> More work needs to be done in emphasising that the only legitimations for arms transfers from the non-pacifist perspective are the preservation of peace, the defence of human rights and the preservation of life and dignity. From a Christian perspective, the concern for the protection of human rights must surely take precedence over arms sales ... This is quite clearly *not* a platform on which a contem-porary British political party could get elected. There is not a consensus of that kind – even against arms sales to highly questionable governments. One task facing the churches is thus the creation of a moral climate in which there is a strong presumption *against* arms sales unless a legitimate need for their transfer can be proven.[12]

The last few years may have seen more public discussion of an ethical policy on arms trade (however flawed) than Williamson anticipated in 1992. Nevertheless, his overall point remains. He believes that churches should become much more active in attempting to change the prevailing moral climate: challenging

---

[12] Roger Williamson, *Profit Without Honour?*, p. 184.

unethical investments; monitoring and lobbying politicians; networking effectively for peace; encouraging a longer-term acceptance of alternatives to warfare; and engaging in a distinctly more critical dialogue on the ethics of arms trade and transfer.

In the last five years a group of twenty-three American theologians and international relations theorists have been meeting to produce a more systematic approach to peace-making in the modern, globalized world. They have now published their initial conclusions in the stimulating book *Just Peacemaking*.[13] They share a common conviction that both pacifist and just-war Christians should make a sustained attempt to promote strategies of peacemaking. Together they identify the following 'ten practices for abolishing war' – practices which specifically include arms reduction:

- Support non-violent direct action.
- Take independent initiatives to reduce threat.
- Use cooperative conflict resolution.
- Acknowledge responsibility for conflict and injustice and seek repentance and forgiveness.
- Advance democracy, human rights, and religious liberty.
- Foster just and sustainable economic development.
- Work with emerging cooperative forces in the inter-national system.
- Strengthen the United Nations and international efforts for cooperation and human rights.
- Reduce offensive weapons and weapons trade.
- Encourage grass-roots peacemaking groups.

If just-war theory in the future really does insist that peaceful means of settlement must not be allowed to fail, then the very use of weapons becomes a clear signal of that failure. One response to arms proliferation is to insist upon the right of everyone to own arms. Libertarian Americans have long insisted upon their personal right to carry arms and the result, many believe, has been one of the most heavily armed and dangerous civilian populations in the world. A quite different response is to work hard for radical decommissioning and peacemaking. From this perspective, a world containing fewer weapons will be a safer world for all of us. Since I share this perspective, I regard much of the present arms trade and transfer as deeply questionable.

[13] Glen Stassen (ed.), *Just Peacemaking: Ten Practices for Abolishing War*, (Cleveland, Ohio: Pilgrim Press, 1999).

3

Media Ethics and the Lambeth Conference

The media typically focus upon issues of morality or practice rather than belief at Lambeth Conferences. When the Anglican bishops gathered for the Lambeth Conference in 1920 and 1930 the issue of contraception in the West received particular attention. A generation later it was the issue of polygamy in Africa that provoked controversy, with some controversy also following the formation of the Church of North India. In 1988 it was the issue of the ordination of women, and the possibility of a widespread exodus to the Roman Catholic or Orthodox Churches, that attracted media interest. In 1998 it could have been one of three issues: women bishops, international debt or homosexuality. The organizers of Lambeth '98 strongly believed that the focus should be on international debt, but feared that it might instead be on women bishops. In the event it was almost exclusively on homosexuality.

As a theological consultant at Lambeth '98, I was able to observe this changing focus at first hand. Naturally, this chapter will be careful not to betray confidences and to use only information that is already in the public domain. However, since I was responsible for drafting and redrafting several of the preparation documents in the ethics section of Lambeth '98 (including that on sexuality), and then for giving advice as the final documents were prepared by the bishops, my interpretation of publicly available information may not always agree with that of others.

The preparation documents for Lambeth '98 were written at a special consultation, which met in London in April 1997. As a preparation for this consultation bishops, meeting in nine provincial areas around the world, were asked to submit reports identifying the main issues that they believed should be given attention at the Conference. Remarkably, all nine areas

34

mentioned international debt as a crucial issue and only three areas (none from the West) mentioned homosexuality. As a result, the preparation conference decided very early that international debt would be given a major plenary session, whereas sexuality would be the subject of a sub-section report but not a plenary session. There was little enthusiasm for making the issue of women bishops the subject of any session or report at all. The bishop with overall responsibility for the ethics sub-sections at Lambeth '98, Archbishop Ngugane of Cape Town, who is known to be sympathetic towards women and gay clergy, is a leading campaigner on international debt and gave a key paper on the subject at Southwark Cathedral while the preparation consultation was meeting. He was determined that it, and not homosexuality or women bishops, should be the main focus of Lambeth '98. Accordingly, a special Christian Aid video on international debt was commissioned for the Conference, a budget set aside to invite the President of the World Bank to address the plenary session, and this sub-section most fully resourced with theological consultants.

Naturally there was still some nervousness about the issue of women bishops. There had already been media speculation that this would again become a divisive issue. At Lambeth '88 there seemed to be a real possibility that either the ordination or the consecration of women would precipitate schism within the Anglican Communion. Archbishop Robert Runcie was widely credited with taking sufficient care to avoid such schism at the time, but a suspicion remained that a divisive debate had merely been postponed at Lambeth '88 and would soon be ignited at Lambeth '98. Those opposed to the ordination of women had already made alternative provision for worship at Lambeth '98 and there was speculation that many might not come at all, especially if women bishops were involved in the opening service. In the event, only three bishops refused to attend the conference on this ground, and although a woman bishop was involved in the ministry of the word in the opening service only a very small group of bishops present refused to communicate. The alternative services at the Conference went ahead without much public controversy, and the media gave little attention either to the ordination or consecration of women.

Why was this? Part of the credit, I believe, should go to the eleven women bishops themselves. Precisely because this was such a non-issue at Lambeth '98, little public credit has been given to them. As so often when successful non-confrontational action is taken, it goes largely unnoticed. In fact several of the women bishops played key roles at different points in the Conference, yet they were always scrupulous in being thoughtful, helpful and eirenic. In addition to the intercessions in the televised Cathedral service which opened the Conference, a woman bishop gave an address at the plenary session on international debt, most were active in the various sub-sections and the Bishop of Edmonton, Victoria Matthews, chaired the plenary session at which Archbishop Rowan Williams gave his keynote lecture on moral decision making. Although they constituted less than two per cent of the bishops present at Lambeth '98, their profile was much higher. A more cautious approach by the organizers might have been to give women bishops no public roles at this Conference at all, waiting instead for the next Lambeth Conference. However, because of the positive role of the women bishops, the approach adopted probably worked rather more successfully.

Of course the style of the women bishops themselves may not have been the only factor involved. As will be seen in a moment, the sheer dominance of the homosexuality debate meant that few other issues were likely to receive media attention. In addition, although women bishops were still relatively uncommon around the Anglican Communion, especially outside North America, a growing number of provinces had already accepted the ordination of women and were now less suspicious of their consecration. In that respect, Lambeth '98 was very different from Lambeth '88. Despite the rumours, there was no longer any serious prospect of schism on this issue and much of the debate had shifted away from schism to alternative provision for those who could not accept women as priests or as bishops. Although all of these factors were probably important, I am still convinced that the women bishops themselves did much to advance their cause at Lambeth '98. In previous Lambeth Conferences, exclusively male bishops argued about the propriety of women's ordination and consecration. In contrast, Lambeth '98, as the first Lambeth Conference able to include women bishops, did not debate the issue at all.

It soon became evident at Lambeth '98 that it was international debt and homosexuality which were the real rivals for media attention. The dynamics between these two issues at the Conference were far more complex than the dynamics of the issue of women bishops. Given the location of the world's poorest and most heavily indebted countries, it was overwhelmingly in the interests of most African, South American and many Asian bishops that international debt should be the main public issue of the Conference. Yet, as the Conference proceeded, most of the bishops came to the conclusion that homosexuality was the key issue and that the final Conference resolutions on this issue constituted a major victory over the liberal West for their provinces. To understand how this happened it is essential to analyse some of the different alliances amongst the bishops and how these played out in a context of considerable media attention.

As already mentioned, the Archbishop of Cape Town was determined that international debt should receive as much exposure to the media as possible. After giving his address at Southwark Cathedral, he appeared on British television to explain the issue further. He chose a publicist from Jubilee 2000 as one of the theological consultants for both the consultation and the Lambeth Conference itself and he planned at length the way that the Lambeth bishops might publicize the issue further. The plenary session at Lambeth '98 was also designed more as an exposition and an inspiration to public action than as a forum for debate amongst the bishops. A high-powered meeting of senior bishops and politicians was planned in London on the day that all of the bishops visited Lambeth and Buckingham Palaces. Finally, Archbishop Ngugane aimed to promote the issue of international debt further at the Assembly of the World Council of Churches meeting later in the year at Harare.

Unfortunately for these plans, Peter Tatchell and his activist gay and lesbian group *Outrage!* were organizing a different media campaign. Equipped with surprisingly accurate information, he and a few other members of *Outrage!* climbed over the back fence at Lambeth Palace, crossed the lawn and disrupted the publicity photograph being taken of the bishops and theological consultants at the outset of the preparation consultation. Instead of the official photograph being published in the broadsheets next day, the photograph taken by *Outrage!*, showing an angry Archbishop Carey confronted by the protesters, appeared instead. On the following Sunday, *Outrage!* disrupted the Sung Eucharist attended by most of the participants at the consultation. However, since Archbishop Carey was this time not present, this protest received little media attention. In the following year, Peter Tatchell and other members of *Outrage!* disrupted Archbishop Carey's Easter Day sermon in Canterbury Cathedral – once again receiving considerable publicity in the national newspapers, radio and television.

Naturally these protests generated much fear amongst the organizers of Lambeth '98 that *Outrage!* might stage a similar protest at the Conference. Not only was such a protest likely to anger many of the bishops, but it might also distract media attention away from the issue of international debt. The University of Kent, at which the last three Lambeth Conferences have been held, has an open campus, which makes the control of any outside groups exceedingly difficult. The tight security that dominated the plenary sessions at Lambeth '98 – understandably the subject of complaint by several journalists – was largely the product of this fear. Yet, with their publicity campaign against the bishops already so effective, *Outrage!* did not actually need to protest on the campus. They had already scared the bishops and ensured that homosexuality would be a dominant issue at the Conference. Given their confrontational approach, it may even have served their purpose better to expose, rather than convert, the bishops. After all, in their previous campaigns their message had been that Anglican bishops were either hypocrites, who needed to be exposed as closet homosexuals, or homophobes.

Another public confrontation on homosexuality was also occurring on the Internet. This confrontation was between the bishops themselves as they prepared for Lambeth '98. It was already clear that most of the American and Canadian bishops did not want this to become a divisive issue at the Conference and were determined to be as non-confrontational as possible. It was noticeable that, even when provoked by anti-American statements made by other bishops at Lambeth '98, ECUSA bishops seldom responded. Under their new and diplomatic presiding bishop, they were fully aware of criticism that had been levelled at them in earlier Lambeth Conferences and were determined, like the women bishops amongst them, to behave with restraint. Here again, little credit has been given them for this.

However, the less controllable Bishop Jack Spong from Newark did use the Internet to publicize his controversial views on moral and doctrinal issues (including that of sexuality). Although he was a restrained member of the sexuality sub-section at the Conference itself, he nevertheless made a series of television broadcasts in the intervals at the Conference. Evangelical bishops from ECUSA, the Southern Cone and Sydney were particularly angry about these broadcasts and his Internet statements. Frequently they cited these as one of the main reasons for raising the public profile of homosexuality as an issue at Lambeth '98.

In view of the different levels of early publicity given to these two issues, it is perhaps not surprising that homosexuality was likely to submerge international debt at Lambeth '98. It mattered little which of the two issues required more theological attention or which might have brought most benefit to a poor and debt-ridden world. The media find public controversy irresistible, and homosexuality was already generating controversy before Lambeth '98 even started. However, once the Conference was under way another factor soon became evident. Since I have already analysed this in the last chapter of my *Churchgoing and Christian Ethics* I can be briefer at this point.

Having examined at some length the reports and resolutions on sexuality, first at Lambeth '88 and then at Lambeth '98, I concluded as follows:

> ... a process is clear. The broad setting and nonprescriptive character of the 1988 Conference report and resolutions have been replaced in the 1998 statement and resolutions with a specific focus upon homosexuality and with a clear normative rejection of homosexual practice as incompatible with Scripture. As a result, the mood of the 1998 Conference and the media attention given to it were inevitably dominated by the issue of homosexuality. Despite the emphasis upon international debt given by the Conference steering committee, by the chair of the ethics section and contained in all nine of the original provincial region reports, this will finally be remembered as the

Conference which sought to reverse years of gradual acceptance of faithful homosexual relationships within parts of the Communion. An inclusive church which already contains many practising homosexual members, as well as homosexual priests and bishops, has adopted a firm moral stance rejecting homosexual practice.[1]

I argued that this process depended upon a highly effective, well-funded and skilfully organized intra-communion, or inter-church, movement (ICM). An ICM, whether within a denomination or across different denominations, is one of the most effective ways that Christians who differ from some widely accepted position within their own denomination on a contentious issue can gather with others for support and to oppose it. Christian pacifists have long adopted this strategy to oppose the dominant non-pacifist positions of most of their fellow Christians. Josephine Butler's challenges to the Contagious Diseases Acts of the nineteenth century, and modern-day opponents of revised liturgies, have also done the same. Lambeth '98 witnessed, perhaps for the first time, an ICM that forged alliances between Western evangelicals and a majority of African and Asian bishops. At the Conference itself, the Oxford Centre for Mission Studies was an essential broker of this ICM. Even though their direct experience and under-standing of homosexuality differed very considerably, the ICM managed to gain the support of two-thirds of the Lambeth bishops (the crucial amendment proposed by the Archbishop of Tanzania, adding the phrase 'while rejecting homosexual practice as incompatible with Scripture' to the resolutions, was supported by 389 bishops and rejected by 190).

The focus of this chapter is specifically upon the media and ethics, so it is worth noting just how useful an ICM is to the media (*Churchgoing and Christian Ethics* provides a more detailed account of the ICM itself). Positively, the media play an indispensable role in raising moral awareness in the general public. Negatively, while doing this they typically polarize and thereby distort moral, and especially theological, issues. An

---

[1] *Churchgoing and Christian Ethics* (Cambridge: Cambridge University Press, 1999), p. 252.

ICM is so effective in media terms precisely because it offers a sharply polarized perspective.

The positive role of the media and ethics is important. Journalists are particularly skilled at presenting complex and technical issues in accessible forms. In a fast-changing and ever more specialized world, all of us depend upon skilled journalists if we are to be properly informed. If we are to make thoughtful moral decisions about complex issues, we do need the information mediated through journalists in subjects other than our own. The media have become essential parts of informed moral decision making. An obvious example of this is in the area of genetics. The mapping of the human genome, the arrival of genetic screening, the genetic modification of food, the possibilities of gene therapy and, perhaps, gene surgery, are all issues of immense complexity. A few years ago we might have been able to regard them as issues for the experts alone, yet now we are becoming aware that they actually affect the daily choices most of us have to make. Genetically modified food has already arrived and we are faced with decisions about it whenever we enter a supermarket. Genetic screening is likely to affect an increasing number of those seeking insurance, mortgages, private health care, and perhaps even employment. Daunting ethical decisions are thereby raised for which accurate information is essential. The prospect of altering human genetic inheritance – if only for those with fatal genetic diseases – raises even more perplexing ethical issues. Informed public knowledge, gleaned largely through the media, is essential if these issues are to be faced responsibly.

This positive moral feature of the media can be found in many areas. Through good journalism we are better informed today about the environment, world poverty, world health care, and many other global issues. We may or may not behave better than our forebears, but we are better informed. Wise moral decision making cannot be ill informed.

Yet it is precisely at this point that the negative feature of journalism obtrudes. Perhaps it is a product of oppositional politics in a liberal democracy. Or perhaps it results simply from a desire to capture our attention. Whatever the reason, journalism tends to polarize the opinions and views it presents. In the interests of 'balance', one view is presented alongside its opposite and an ICM presents an easily accessible means of doing this. Ironically, really balanced views tend to be ignored in the process. Media 'balance', in other words, is often created more by the juxtaposition of unbalanced views than by the presentation of balanced ones.

Scholars at the receiving end of journalists will be well aware of this process. A journalist rings politely asking for your views about X. You explain your views with careful qualifications. 'But you do think Y, professor, don't you?' is the typical response. 'Well, no I don't: it is more complex than that, as I have just explained.' Listening to a conversation like this in my office, a senior medical academic said afterwards that he regarded talking to journalists as simply a waste of time. 'They don't want careful opinions, but only simplistic positions.' The trap for academics – or indeed for church leaders – who wish to appear as experts in the media is that they must not be balanced. They must present polarized views. And this is precisely what an ICM does.

Being at the receiving end of a well-organized ICM at Lambeth '98, I was only too aware that it depended less upon internal logic or theology than upon ecclesiastical politics in a media context. The alliances forged within it on homosexuality were considerably more fragile in other areas of sexuality. For example, those bishops from Dallas and Sydney, who were instrumental in this ICM, were themselves thoroughly divided on the issue of remarriage after divorce. Bishops from Central Africa were anxious not to include any reference to the divisive issue of polygamy (tolerated by previous Lambeth Conferences as a passing phenomenon, but in reality still present in several parts of Africa) and, while condemning cohabitation in the West, were often supportive of traditional African marriage. I gradually came to the conclusion that there was no other area of human sexuality that united members of this ICM against their opponents. Even amongst the 389 bishops who supported the Archbishop of Tanzania's amendment, some conflated homosexuality with paedophilia and even with bestiality, some wanted to include references to homosexual 'healing', some wished to condemn homosexual orientation as well as practice, and some dissented strongly from all of these.

Given these three media-related factors – the campaign of *Outrage!*, the debate on the Internet, and this ICM – it is perhaps no longer surprising that homosexuality rather than international debt became the major public issue at Lambeth '98. And this happened despite international debt being the issue that apparently united the bishops at the outset and that most affected the lives of two-thirds of the Anglicans represented at the Conference.

However, there may have been another factor involved in the complicated politics of Lambeth '98. It is possible that it was in the interests of some of the bishops to ensure that homosexuality and not international debt became the dominant issue. Since there was such overwhelming support amongst the bishops for cancellation of international debt, at least for the poorest and most heavily indebted countries, it was going to take a brave or foolish bishop publicly to oppose this. As already mentioned, the plenary session on international debt was not designed to foster debate, and the eventual Conference report on this issue contained remarkably few of the ten conditions for debt cancellation advocated in Archbishop Ngugane's Southwark lecture. And yet some of the bishops from entrepreneurial cultures, especially within the south of the United States and parts of Far East Asia, were known to be unhappy about supporting debt cancellation in any form. Whether deliberately or not, their strong support for the ICM on homosexuality took away media attention from international debt. This may well have suited them, although surely it could hardly have suited the bishops from poor and heavily indebted countries. Distraction can be an effective tactic in a media age.

Finally, it is interesting to speculate a little about the next Lambeth Conference. Is there another issue of morality or practice that might divide the bishops in the future and attract the attention of the media? It is risky to make predictions but my own view is that this is unlikely. However, I suspect that the issue of the ordination or consecration of women is now a non-issue for future Lambeth Conferences and that, in this respect, Lambeth '98 will come to be seen as a watershed. It is difficult to imagine any reversal of the decision to admit women to ordained ministry. In addition, the more provinces there are that ordain and consecrate women the less likely is schism on this account within the Anglican Communion. At the level of Lambeth Conferences, this is now most unlikely to be an issue that ever again dominates agendas.

What about homosexuality? Some have speculated that this could cause further schism among Anglicans at a future Lambeth Conference. As I write, the newly formed Anglican Mission in America does seem to be moving in a schismatic direction. Yet it remains to be seen how far this will go in this direction. There may well be future resolutions at Lambeth Conferences confirming the Lambeth '98 resolution 'rejecting homosexual practice as incompatible with Scripture', but this will hardly surprise the minority of, largely Western, bishops who dissented from it. There may be future threats from those opposing homosexuality that they will break away from a Church that still has provinces tacitly or explicitly supporting gay or lesbian priests. Yet, in a Church lacking a centralized authority, it is usually the minority that leaves the majority, not the majority that breaks away from the minority.

What about the authority of Scripture? This was certainly an important topic at Lambeth '98, as the homosexuality amendment indicates. Many theologians who acted as consultants at Lambeth '98 came away from it distressed at the general level of theological debate and biblical understanding amongst the bishops. Perhaps, given the uneven patterns of theological education now available across the Anglican Communion, this is not too surprising. Doubtless there is considerable scope here for controversies and antagonisms at future Lambeth Conferences. Yet, in a sense, these have characterized Christians from the outset and Anglicans have always struggled to contain divergent approaches to Scripture.

It could easily be an issue of practice rather than morality that divides the next Lambeth Conference. Lay presidency at the eucharist is an obvious candidate. Nevertheless, it is difficult to imagine this issue inspiring much media attention. Pressure already seems to be increasing to move the Lambeth Conference away from Canterbury and Lambeth altogether. In that case, it may follow the rotating path of the Assemblies of the World Council of Churches and become a world event that, ironically, is ignored by most of the world's media.

4

Sexual Ethics

Whether or not sexual ethics actually causes schism within the Anglican Church or within other mainstream denominations, there can be little doubt that it is likely to remain troublesome and intractable. Unlike some of the highly complex areas of biotechnology that affect the few, or the daunting issues of macroeconomics that affect us all but seem beyond individual control, sexual ethics impinges upon the personal lives of almost everyone. Decisions about personal sexual behaviour, and strong moral attitudes about the sexual behaviour of others, seem to be part of the human condition. Attempts to regulate this behaviour and shape these attitudes can be found in many religious traditions, and especially within the Christian tradition, yet because of the evident changes within both the Church and society at large in the second half of the twentieth century, the twenty-first century seems likely to bring considerable tensions and debates.

There is a real need to analyse the present situation carefully before offering any prescriptions for the future. This chapter will try to do this. However, a warning is necessary at the outset. Although it has long been a practice in Anglican ethics to present an empirical analysis of an issue first before turning to theology and Christian ethics, this practice has come under increasing attack.[1] Indeed, it presents an obvious danger. The empirical 'is' can easily dictate the theological 'ought'; secular practice can determine theological vision; and, in the process, the distinctiveness of Christian ethics can simply be lost. Christian ethics becomes, in effect, a means of legitimating secular moral (or immoral) practices.

---

[1] See, for example, Alistair McFadyen's stimulating *Bound to Sin: Abuse, Holocaust and the Christian Doctrine of Sin* (Cambridge: Cambridge University Press, 2000).

To avoid this, it is essential to emphasize that this is not my intention here. Instead, the first part of this chapter will seek to understand why Anglicans are both changing and increasingly confused about sexual ethics. There is no assumption here that all of these changes are desirable, or even undesirable, in terms of Christian ethics. The final part of the chapter will move from this analytic mode to a more theological and prescriptive mode, searching for theological principles that might unite most Anglicans despite our evident differences. This theological reconstruction, as so often elsewhere in Christian ethics, is considerably more difficult than the analytic task.

Two Reports

That Anglicans are both changing and increasingly confused about sexual ethics (alongside most other mainstream denominations) is evident from two reports produced in the 1990s. The first of these was the 1991 House of Bishops' *Issues in Human Sexuality*.[2] In his preface, the then new Archbishop of Canterbury admitted that there was 'a wide variety of opinions even amongst the Bishops on the issue of homosexuality'. He modestly encouraged congregations 'to find time for prayerful study and reflection on the issues we have discussed' and made no claim that this would be 'the last word on the subject'. The second report appeared four years later and was surrounded by considerable media attention, namely *Something to Celebrate*[3] produced by a working party of the Board for Social Responsibility. This second report was commended in a foreword by the then Bishops of Liverpool and Bath and Wells, both of whom had been present at the discussions that produced the first report. They wrote hoping that 'it will prove to be a rich resource for debate across the country', but also warning that 'not every member of the Board would want to support every specific approach that appears here, but all agree that this is a positive contribution to the debate which will

---

[2] *Issues in Human Sexuality: A Statement by the House of Bishops of the General Synod of the Church of England* (London: Church House Publishing, 1991).
[3] *Something to Celebrate: Valuing Families in Church and Society* (London: Church House Publishing, 1995).

encourage widespread reflection and action. *Something to Celebrate* is a resource for Church and society.'

However, the eirenic tone of both of these opening recommendations has done little to resolve the divisions that prompted the reports in the first place – divisions that, as just seen in the previous chapter, were soon to resurface at the Lambeth Conference. Both reports well illustrate just how intractable sexual ethics currently seems to be, especially for a broad Church such as the Church of England. *Issues in Human Sexuality* was prompted in the first place by the obvious fact that gay priests and laypeople, who have long been present especially within the Anglo-Catholic wing of the Church of England, have recently become less covert about their sexual behaviour. *Something to Celebrate* was prompted by the fact that the children of many practising Anglicans (clergy and laity), some younger practising Anglicans themselves, and even some of the younger clergy, were already cohabiting outside of marriage. Herein lay the central existential problem for both reports; actual practice did not accord with current theory even within the Church. (Once again, it is important to emphasize that this is an analytical point and says nothing at this stage about whether such practice should be condemned, condoned or simply tolerated.)

Faced with these existential problems the two reports responded rather differently, although ironically both were criticized for the way they reacted. *Issues in Human Sexuality* argued that although faithful but active homosexual relationships between lay Christians might be condoned, those between clergy could not be. The bishops argued:

> We have, therefore, to say that in our considered judgement the clergy cannot claim the liberty to enter into sexually active homophile relationships. Because of the distinctive nature of their calling, status and consecration, to allow such a claim on their part would be seen as placing that way of life in all respects on a par with heterosexual marriage as a reflection of God's purposes in creation. The Church cannot accept such a parity and remain faithful to the insights which God has given it through Scripture, tradition and reasoned reflection on experience.[4]

[4] *Issues in Sexuality*, 5.17.

Clearly an underlying belief here is that clergy should be subject to higher professional standards than laypeople and, indeed, many clergy may well accept such a belief. The secrecy of the confessional and the imperative to maintain non-sexual relationships with those under their care are ethical require-ments for several professional groups. Doctors, for example, are just as adamant about the need for patient confidentiality and for non-exploitative doctor–patient relationships (curi-ously, university academics remain ambivalent about both). But why, several theologians asked, should any of this refer to homosexual behaviour, especially if it is faithful and does not exploit parishioners? The answer in the paragraph just quoted seems to be that sanctioning active homosexuality amongst the clergy 'would be seen as placing that way of life in all respects on a par with heterosexual marriage as a reflection of God's purposes in creation'. But why, the same theologians asked, does this consideration apply especially to the clergy? Does it not apply equally to laypeople?

Having put this argument, the bishops at once insisted that it would be wrong for them as bishops to be 'rigorous in searching out and exposing clergy who may be in sexually active homophile relationships'.[5] They argued that it is wrong to assume that all those who cohabit have an active sexual relationship and that it would be wrong to carry out intrusive interrogations amongst the clergy. They concluded:

> Although we must take steps to avoid public scandal and to protect the Church's teaching, we shall continue, as we have done hitherto, to treat all clergy who give no occasion for scandal with trust and respect, and we expect all our fellow Christians to do the same.[6]

Critics soon identified this as the crucial chink in the bishops' argument. They had admitted their internal differences, but had united in their concern about 'public scandal'. Logically, their argument allowed for private homosexual behaviour amongst the clergy as long as this behaviour never became a matter of public scandal. Cynics soon interpreted this as an

[5] *Issues in Sexuality*, 5.18.
[6] *Issues in Sexuality*, 5.18.

injunction not to be found out. It mirrored Max Weber's concept of 'perceived honesty' when he argued[7] that at the heart of the spirit of Western capitalism lay a novel combination of hard work, thrift and perceived honesty. Hard-working and thrifty capitalists would not be trusted with the capital of others unless they were *perceived* by the latter to be honest. If they were privately honest but publicly suspected of being dishonest, they would be as badly placed in business terms as capitalists who were both privately and publicly dishonest. In contrast, successful capitalists might be either privately and publicly honest or privately dishonest but perceived in public to be honest. In the rise of Western capitalism, so Weber argued, public perception became the dominant variable. Thus, bizarrely, honesty became a functional commodity and its normal moral meaning became inverted – somewhat like versions of 'ostentatious humility' which are important for promotion in many hierarchical but non-democratic organizations (including some churches).

In a similar way, homosexual ordinands in faithful but sexually active relationships soon realized that, if they were to be ordained, they would be unwise to tell their ordaining bishop. The latter appeared most concerned about the avoidance of 'public scandal'. But, critics continued, does this not encourage just the sort of hypocrisy that is most detested by secular society (and which, of course, Jesus in the Synoptic Gospels persistently criticized)? Just this has been one of the most damaging areas for the Roman Catholic Church on the issue of clerical celibacy. An ideal is upheld despite widespread evidence that in some parts of the world many, perhaps even a majority of, priests do not uphold it and despite a series of very damning instances of Western priests and bishops leading double lives. Only when such cases become public scandals do they characteristically receive public reprimand. Ecclesiastical hierarchies would usually rather deal with what they deem to be clerical and, sometimes, episcopal sexual misbehaviour – even illegal forms of misbehaviour such as paedophilia – with private reprimands and, if necessary,

---

[7] Max Weber, *The Protestant Ethic and the 'Spirit' of Capitalism* (London: Unwin, 1930).

career moves. Only when this behaviour becomes public – usually because of reports in the media – is further action typically taken. In other words, the dominant concern is to avoid public revelations, especially in the media, and, thus, public scandal – and it is just this which is often identified in society at large today as public hypocrisy.

Further, the critics continued, which public is it that might be scandalized? This question raises the important issue of possible changes in public opinion, to which I shall turn in a moment. *Issues in Human Sexuality* did little to resolve these critical questions.

Something to Celebrate raised rather different critical questions. Ostensibly the working party that wrote this report supported the bishops' report. For example, having briefly set out their views on homosexuality, they concluded:

> We therefore support the House of Bishops' hope that there will be a continuing growth in understanding and support of gay and lesbian people and a fuller integration of all that they may be able to teach and give through their own particular perspective.[8]

However, they avoided the vexed issue of clerical homosexuality and with it the argument of the bishops that condoning it 'would be seen as placing that way of life in all respects on a par with heterosexual marriage'. Indeed, they annoyed their critics precisely by appearing to put cohabitation – heterosexual and perhaps even homosexual – almost on a par with marriage. For example, they argued that 'the wisest and most practical way forward ... may be for Christians both to hold fast to the centrality of marriage and at the same time to accept that cohabitation is, for many people, a step along the way towards that fuller and more complete commitment'.[9] A little later they claimed that 'some forms of cohabitation are marriages already in all but name ... in terms of the theology of marriage, cohabitation which involves a mutual, life-long, exclusive commitment may be a legitimate form of marriage, what might be called "pre-ceremonial" or "without ceremonial" marriage'.[10]

[8] *Something to Celebrate*, p. 121.
[9] *Something to Celebrate*, p. 115.
[10] *Something to Celebrate*, p. 116.

And a few pages later, they argued that many gay and lesbian partnerships also involve 'commitment and interdependence' and 'are able to create relationships of high quality, capable of expressing love, joy, peace, faithfulness, endurance, self-sacrifice and service to the outside world beyond their relationship'.[11] They believed encouragement and support, rather than condemnation, to be the appropriate Christian responses to these 'families'.

Some of the critics of the report caricatured it as little more than a legitimation of secular sexual practices. In reality, the authors of the report argued in several places that the 'Christian practice of lifelong, monogamous marriage lies at the heart of the Church's understanding of how the love of God is made manifest in the sexual companionship of a man and a woman'.[12] At the same time, they did not wish to condemn those who differed from this position:

> The widespread practice of cohabitation needs to be attended to with sympathy and discernment, especially in the light of the enormous changes in western society that have taken place recently and the effect these have had on the understanding and practice of personal relationships. Anxiety amongst churchgoers about cohabitation is best allayed, not by judgemental attitudes about 'fornication' and 'living in sin', but by the confident celebration of marriage and the affirmation and support of what in cohabiting relationships corresponds most with the Christian ideal. Being disapproving and hostile towards people who cohabit only leads to alienation and a breakdown in communications. Instead, congregations should welcome cohabitees, listen to them, learn from them and co-operate with them so that all may discover God's presence in their lives and in our own, at the same time as bearing witness to that sharing in God's love which is also available within marriage.[13]

The authors of *Something to Celebrate* argued with some passion that 'too often the Church has been censorious and

[11] *Something to Celebrate*, p. 120.
[12] *Something to Celebrate*, p. 118.
[13] *Something to Celebrate*, p. 118.

judgemental in matters of personal ethics' and considered that 'the beginning of a meeting of minds and hearts is only likely to occur if the Church is honest about its failure to embody the love of God in its teaching and practice of marriage and family life'.[14] In contrast to the bishops, the working party was less concerned about public scandal affecting the Church and more about what they considered to be anachronistic attitudes within the Church. They wrote, perhaps, more as the Christian parents of young adults in a changing society, than as bishops concerned with the Church's public reputation. The differing social contexts of the House of Bishops and the Board of Social Responsibility may well have contributed to this crucial difference.

Not surprisingly, they attracted rather different critics. Nevertheless, and this is important for my analysis, both of these predominantly eirenic and non-confrontational reports did attract vehement critics, within and outside the Church. If the first was considered to be too arbitrary in setting different standards on homosexual behaviour for laity and clergy (despite the known presence of a substantial number of actively gay clergy in parts of the Church), the second was considered to be too devoid of Christian standards (despite the evident differences amongst Anglicans on most sexual issues). The two reports certainly did not represent the full spectrum of sexual attitudes in the Church of England – for some the bishops were still far too liberal and for others the working party was too conservative. Together, they illustrate some of the deep divisions to be found in many countries amongst Anglicans at the end of the twentieth century – divisions that will surely continue to trouble us and members of other mainstream denominations in the twenty-first century. To understand these adequately it is important to understand their broader context. It is to this that I must turn next.

Changing Attitudes

The clearest feature of this broader context is that, for better or worse, social attitudes about sexual ethics radically changed in

---

[14] *Something to Celebrate*, p. 115.

the second half of the twentieth century. It is obvious that this has happened, but it may be less obvious that the attitudes of churchgoers, although somewhat more conservative than those of the general population, do seem to be changing fast as well. Clergy attitudes change too, but more slowly than other groups. Frequently it is claimed that 'liberal' clergy have been responsible for these changes among churchgoers. From this perspective clergy, fashioned by the relativism of liberal theology and critical biblical studies, have become agents of secularization within the Church. This claim is frequently made, but it has seldom been made on the basis of any reliable empirical research.

Again, as I maintained earlier in chapter 1, testing such claims against opinion-poll data has been central to my recent research, reported in detail in *Churchgoing and Christian Ethics*.[15] This research suggests that the reverse may in reality be the case – on sexual issues most clergy are more conservative than their congregations and change their opinions on these issues some decades later. Of course opinion polls cannot clarify everything, especially in areas as complex as attitudes to sexual ethics. Nonetheless, they do show a remarkable consistency when set out longitudinally and compared in different areas.

It is not necessary to rehearse all of the evidence given at length in *Churchgoing and Christian Ethics*. Here I will simply summarize some of the main findings as they apply to British churches.

For a number of years, opinion polls have asked people whether or not divorcees should be allowed to marry in church. So, back in 1947, a Gallup Poll[16] found that 34 per cent of the general public thought that they should not and 58 per cent that they should. However, by 1955 only 28 per cent thought that they should not, and by 1984 just 24 per cent. Yet despite this widespread general acceptance that divorcees should be allowed to marry in church, a majority of

[15] Cambridge: Cambridge University Press, 1999.

[16] Gallup Opinion Poll data can be found in George H. Gallup, *The Gallup International Public Opinion Polls: Great Britain 1937–1975*, Vols. 1 & 2 (New York: Random House, 1976); in *The International Gallup Polls* (Gallup Organization, 1978); and in *The Gallup Political Index* (Gallup Organization, published annually).

'communicant churchgoers' in 1955 were opposed, with 55 per cent believing that they should not and only 37 per cent that they should. An opinion poll conducted by the BBC[17] in December 1954 also showed a very similar, sharp difference of attitude on divorce between churchgoers and the general public: 53 per cent of those who reported that they went to church 'most Sundays' thought that the divorce laws should be made stricter, whereas only 30 per cent of the general public held this view. However, by 1984 there was a very significant change. Now Gallup found that 55 per cent of churchgoers were in favour of divorcees being allowed to marry in church and only 29 per cent were opposed. Yet opposition remained strong among clergy: 44 per cent of Anglican clergy were opposed and only 21 per cent in support. Nevertheless, by 1994 another poll[18] found that Anglican clergy opposition had dropped to 32 per cent and a 1996 Gallup Poll found that it was now only 28 per cent.

It is important not to exaggerate this evidence. In *Churchgoing and Christian Ethics* I present complex data using the *British Social Attitudes* survey showing that regular churchgoers remain more opposed than irregular churchgoers or non-churchgoers to the liberalization of divorce laws. They are also less likely than others themselves to be divorced. Yet even here there are changes. Divorce is on the increase among regular churchgoers (as it is among Anglican clergy) even if it is still less common than among the general public. Regular churchgoers, clergy children and the clergy themselves (and even bishops) are clearly not immune from changes that are happening in society at large. However much they might deplore these changes they are increasingly caught up in them themselves. It is hardly surprising, then, that their attitudes to the question whether or not divorcees should be allowed to marry in church also change. Yet far from this representing some 'liberal' conspiracy of the clergy, the evidence suggests that clergy as a whole have followed rather than led the views of their congregations. It could well be argued that instead of

[17] British Broadcasting Corporation, *Religious Broadcasts and the Public* (BBC: Audience Research Department, 1955).
[18] Ted Harrison, *Members Only?* (London: Triangle/SPCK, 1994).

being the agents of secularization, it is rather a persistent pastoral demand that has persuaded them to change.

A second area studied at length in *Churchgoing and Christian Ethics* is that of attitudes towards both sex before marriage and cohabitation. A similar pattern emerges in an area that, in this case, shows a very considerable shift in public opinion. As recently as 1964, Gallup found that 64 per cent of the general public (and 79 per cent of Anglican churchgoers) did not approve of sex before marriage. However, by 1978 those who did not approve in the general population had reduced to just 26 per cent. *British Social Attitudes* mapped a subsequent change: in 1983 *BSA* found that 42 per cent responded that sex before marriage was simply 'not wrong' and 28 per cent that it was 'always or mostly wrong', whereas in 1993 this had changed to 54 per cent and 18 per cent respectively. Interestingly, Leslie Francis[19] in 1995 found that among those aged 13–15, just 22 per cent of churchgoing Anglicans and 30 per cent of church-going Roman Catholics thought that sex before marriage was 'always or mostly wrong'. *BSA* also found in 1993 that 64 per cent of the general public approved of couples living together without intending to get married. Similarly, in 1996 Gallup found that 68 per cent of the general population and even 56 per cent of adult churchgoers approved. In this last survey it was again the clergy who differed, with only 36 per cent approving of cohabitation.

So once again it appears that Anglican clergy as a whole appear to be more conservative on sexual issues than Anglican laity: the latter, in turn, have followed changes of attitude within the general population. Here, too, nuance is important. *Churchgoing and Christian Ethics* presents complex data here as well, showing that churchgoers *are* more conservative than irregular churchgoers or non-churchgoers. They both approve of cohabitation and cohabit themselves less than the population at large. Nonetheless, they are changing: an increasing proportion of churchgoers have come to accept cohabitation (perhaps because their children cohabit) and, among younger churchgoers at least, cohabit themselves.

---

[19] Leslie J. Francis and William K. Kay, *Teenage Religion and Values* (Leominster: Gracewing/Fowler Wright Books, 1995).

There is a third area that also shows shifting attitudes and clear differences between clergy and laity. Homosexual practice still receives wider condemnation in the public at large than heterosexual practice. Before a change in English law, Gallup in 1957 found that only 38 per cent of the population thought that homosexuality should be decriminalized for adults and, even after the law did change, Gallup in 1964 found that just 36 per cent of churchgoers thought that society should be tolerant of homosexuals. In addition, 50 per cent of the adults in both *BSA* 1983 and 1993 thought that homosexual relations between adults were 'always wrong'. Nevertheless, once again Leslie Francis' 1995 sample of 13–15-year-olds suggests that attitudes here are changing among the young: only 30 per cent of young Anglican churchgoers thought that homosexuality was wrong. Furthermore, a Gallup Poll in 1984 found that only 45 per cent of the adult population thought that the 'Church can never approve homosexual acts', compared with 52 per cent of Anglican laity and 61 per cent of Anglican clergy. A difference in attitudes between Anglican laity and clergy was again found in a survey by *The Guardian* of newly elected General Synod members in 1996 in which 45 per cent of laity and 70 per cent of clergy agreed that the Church could not approve homosexual acts. A difference, albeit a narrower one, with 53 per cent of Anglican churchgoers and 59 per cent of Anglican clergy disapproving, was found in 1996 by Gallup.

Despite this evidence about Anglican clergy being generally more conservative than Anglican laity, it could still be argued that they have failed to offer congregations sufficiently strong and distinctive leadership on sexual issues. This, of course, is a weaker claim than the first. The stronger claim is that a secularized clergy has influenced (misled) the laity, whereas the weaker claim is that a clergy lacking authority or sufficient will has failed to lead the laity away from secular trends.

It is this second claim that Michael Banner seems to make. He compares the Church of England's *Issues in Human Sexuality* unfavourably with the American Roman Catholic bishops' report *Human Sexuality*.[20] The latter has 'a rather distinctive

---

[20] United States Catholic Conference, *Human Sexuality: A Catholic Perspective for Education and Lifelong Learning* (Washington, 1991).

notion of what it is to establish the "mind of Christ", and one more likely, perhaps, to guarantee consistency and clarity if not necessarily truth'.[21] In contrast, he parodies the Anglican plea not to 'reject' laity who are practising homosexuals as follows:

> But, since the Church of England neither excommunicates nor, in effect, imposes any penitential discipline on what it takes to be its erring members, the promise not to reject homosexuals seems to add nothing to existing practice, unless we take it as a welcome signal of a determination to ensure that practising homosexuals are not singled out for the more informal 'discipline' which certain congregations no doubt exercise in excluding some from fellowship. [22]

From this perspective, presumably, strong leadership from the clergy on sexual issues is considered vital to maintain the distinctiveness of Christian ethics amongst churchgoers.

In *Churchgoing and Christian Ethics* I offer empirical evidence about the effectiveness or non-effectiveness of clerical leadership on sexual issues, albeit in the Roman Catholic rather than Anglican Church. Using Gallup Poll data again, it appears that in 1964 (that is, before the publication of *Humanae Vitae*) both the general population and non-Roman Catholic church-goers overwhelmingly approved of contraception within marriage. Two surveys in that year found general support of between 79 per cent and 81 per cent, with this support dropping only slightly to 75 per cent among those attending Free Churches and rising to 85 per cent among Anglican churchgoers. In contrast, only 32 per cent of Roman Catholic churchgoers approved and 59 per cent actively disapproved. Nevertheless, it soon became evident that, despite *Humanae Vitae* and a very firm papal line ever since, sexually active Roman Catholics in many parts of the Western world did resort to contraception (and abortion) in proportionate numbers to other groups in the population at large. So much so that Leslie Francis' 1995 research found that 72 per cent of both Anglican and Roman Catholic teenage churchgoers disagreed with the

---

[21] Michael Banner, *Christian Ethics and Contemporary Moral Problems* (Cambridge: Cambridge University Press, 1999), p. 268.
[22] Banner, *Christian Ethics*, pp. 266–7.

proposition that contraception is wrong. The conclusion to be reached appears obvious:

> In the second half of the 20th century the hierarchy of the Roman Catholic Church has taken a determined, and for some courageous, stand against public opinion on a matter of sexual ethics which affects most sexually active people. Almost alone in any major Christian denomination, this hierarchy has decided to take a stand against prevailing mores and uphold a traditional sexual standard. It may even have done this despite the alienation of many of its own sexually active churchgoers. Yet the evidence suggests that this stand has not substantially altered either the practice of Catholic laity or even the attitudes of young Catholics. Despite one of the most systematic attempts at ecclesiastical teaching and control during this period, Roman Catholic churchgoers now appear little different from the general population in attitudes towards, or practice of, proscribed forms of contraception.[23]

Herein lies the problem for Anglican as well as Roman Catholic bishops in many countries, especially where congregations are disproportionately elderly. It appears that it is the elderly who are especially inclined to believe that homosexuality can never be justified.[24] So for this group, *Issues in Human Sexuality* was likely to be viewed as dangerously liberal, since it did not unambiguously condemn faithful homosexual relationships among laypeople. Yet for most of the young group of church-goers, homosexuality and heterosexual cohabitation are simply not seen as wrong at all. So any attempt by bishops to proscribe homosexual relationships amongst the clergy (let alone cohabitation, whether homosexual or heterosexual, more widely) is always likely to be viewed by this young group as either homophobia or hypocrisy. The middle-aged are likely to sit somewhere between these two perspectives – sharing the ambiguities and confusions of the new millennium.

---

[23] *Churchgoing and Christian Ethics*, p. 161.
[24] For impressive evidence of generational differences in many countries, see Ronald Inglehart, *Culture Shift in Advanced Industrial Society* (New Jersey: Princeton University Press, 1990).

In this context of polarized attitudes, and disregarding for the moment all theological considerations, the English bishops evidently faced a thankless task when they met to produce *Issues in Human Sexuality*. On a divisive issue such as homosexual relationships they could not expect to please all age groups even within their own Church. What appears to be simply wrong to the older age group is likely to be acceptable to the younger group. And on issues where society at large and even a majority of churchgoers have changed their views – for example, on the issue of divorcees marrying in church – they are still likely to encounter strong opposition from many of the clergy. If they take a firm line against popular opinion – as the Roman Catholic hierarchy did on barrier and hormonal forms of contraception – they are likely to alienate the faithful or simply be ignored by them. Yet if they take a more liberal line – as the authors of *Something to Celebrate* did – they are likely to be accused by some within the Church of being agents of secularization. In the circumstances, it may hardly be surprising that *Issues in Human Sexuality* is now widely seen as a deeply contradictory document.

Perhaps theology can rescue this situation.

Theological Divisions

Unfortunately biblical and historical scholars are not always very helpful at this point. Just when it is thought that the unified voice of the Bible or church history on sexual ethics might resolve these contradictions and ambiguities, scholars seem increasingly to stress that distinctively Christian resources are themselves surprisingly pluralistic. The problem seems to be twofold: much modern scholarship appears to present a plurality of both contents and methods. At the contents level, many scholars detect crucial differences of perspective on sexual ethics between the Old and New Testaments and between both of these and subsequent church history. At the methodological level, a wide variety of hermeneutical perspectives makes it seem ever less likely that Christian theologians can reach a consensus, especially on those issues such as sexuality that have crucial gender and cultural implications.

Three recent collections, each with a predominance of Anglican contributors, confirm this situation at the contents level. The first of these collections is *New Occasions Teach New Duties? Christian Ethics for Today*, edited by Cyril S. Rodd.[25] It consists of articles originally written for *The Expository Times* intended to introduce general readers to the current state of scholarship in Christian ethics. This collection opens with two critical articles on biblical ethics. The first, by Cyril Rodd, looks at the use of the Old Testament in Christian ethics, and the second, by Howard Marshall, looks at the use of the New Testament. Both offer many more problems than they resolve (even Marshall, despite his generally conservative position, has surprisingly little positive to say) and present a very effective challenge, which is taken up by several of the authors that follow. If the Bible is indeed the central and most distinctively Christian resource for Christian ethics, then how do we resolve its internal pluralism, its anachronisms, its gaps, and the varying synchronic and diachronic interpretations that are made of it? Alister McGrath boldly compounds these problems by noting key differences amongst the Reformers, and David Brown adds complexities by setting Christian ethics in its present-day context of competing philosophies. Richard Jones instructively looks at the differing ways that individual Christians make decisions (for example, about whether they should or should not be ordained). Alan Suggate, John Atherton and David Cook all offer useful but characteristic accounts of their specialist areas in Christian ethics – namely Church and state, economics and medical ethics. Stephen Barton, fresh from *Something to Celebrate*, offers a gentle piece on sexuality – although I suspect that it will not satisfy his conservative critics. William Storrar looks at the 'option for the poor', Graham Gould at the Church Fathers, and Peter Bishop at issues of war and peace.

The second collection is *The Family in Theological Perspective*, this time edited by Stephen Barton,[26] and the third is *Christian Perspectives on Sexuality and Gender*, edited by Adrian Thatcher and Elizabeth Stuart.[27] Both of these collections compound the plurality of distinctively Christian resources on ethical issues

[25] Edinburgh: T&T Clark, 1995.
[26] Edinburgh: T&T Clark, 1996.
[27] Leominster: Gracewing/Fowler Wright Books, 1996. See also Adrian Thatcher's *Living Together and Christian Ethics* (Cambridge: Cambridge University Press, 2001).

evident in the first collection. Not one of the collections offers any clear path through these differences.

Stephen Barton, featuring prominently in all of the collections, is very much at the centre of the recent debate in the Church of England. In a series of measured articles, he seeks to show some of the difficulties facing those wishing to claim that Christians can speak with a united voice on the family or sexuality. For him, it is not the plurality of present-day society that causes these difficulties but the Bible itself and our relationship to it. He seeks to move readers away from interminable debates about particular biblical texts (for example, the cluster of much-cited verses on homosexuality), and towards a more hermeneutical perspective, seeing us as contextualized late-twentieth-century people coming to the Bible for enlightenment rather than for proof texts. But, of course, therein lies the problem: we already come to the Bible with our gender, ethnic and social class differences.

The Family in Theological Perspective consists of eighteen thoughtful papers originally given to seminars at the Durham Centre for Theological Research. Most of the contributors are academics at Durham or Newcastle University. An exception is John Rogerson who gives a very helpful paper on the family in the Old Testament, set alongside similar papers on the New Testament by James Dunn and James Francis. Carol Harrison, Anthony Fletcher and Sheridan Gilley offer papers on the family in historical perspectives. The second half of this collection is a little more disparate, with contributions amongst others from Peter Selby, Michael Vasey, Jeff Astley, Jon Davies, Alan Suggate and Gerard Loughlin, all of whom have something interesting to add to the debate. However, Susan Parsons presents one of the most cogent papers, outlining the thesis that she sets out so well in her *Feminism and Christian Ethics* [28] on differences between feminists, these often resulting from the crucial issue of whether they consider gender distinctions to be socially or biologically constructed.

Christian Perspectives on Sexuality and Gender is in effect a reader, since all but one of its thirty-six articles have been previously published elsewhere. Whereas half of the second

---

[28] Cambridge: Cambridge University Press, 1996.

collection is concerned with biblical and historical tradition, in the third collection this subject occupies just three articles, by Stephen Barton, Richard Price and Daniel Doriani. Of the other sections, those on power and relation (with characteristic and contrasting contributions from Daphne Hampson and Mary Grey), on sexuality and spirituality (James Nelson), and on sexuality, violence and families (Rosemary Radford Ruether, Stephen Barton and Susan Parsons again) are all interesting. The tone and standard of the contributions in this collection are not as even and scholarly as those in the other two. Nevertheless, the three books work well together and abundantly illustrate the plurality facing the very heart of Christian ethics.

Of course, despite this evident plurality, there might still be a single and distinctively Christian narrative beneath it. If it were possible to discern such an underlying narrative in the Bible on sexual ethics, would this settle the theological debate? The Roman Catholic writer Anne E. Patrick, in her book *Liberating Conscience: Feminist Explorations in Catholic Moral Theology*,[29] argues that it would not, since such a patriarchal biblical narrative would still need correction.

Anne Patrick, SNJM, is Professor of Religion at Carleton College, Minnesota, and a past president of the influential Catholic Theological Society of America. Writing very much as a Catholic for other Catholics, she introduces her first chapter with this quotation: 'When I was young ... there never was any question of right and wrong. We knew our catechism, and that was enough. We learned our creed and our duty. Every respectable church person had the same opinions.'[30] This expresses very well the dilemma of many Roman Catholics today. Once Church authority and morality were firmly anchored, but today, and despite a strong Pope, they are not. In the wake of Bishop Roderick Wright's resignation, even that staunch defender of Catholicism, Clifford Longley, admitted in *The Daily Telegraph* that a Roman Catholic congregation is likely to start collecting for a 'going away present' for a priest who decides to get married. Anne Patrick herself provides

---

[29] London: SCM Press, 1996.
[30] Patrick, *Liberating Conscience*, p. 19.

numerous examples of changing Catholic perceptions and values. Yet she teases her readers, since her quotation is from the last century by George Eliot and refers to Anglicans not to Roman Catholics. Her message is clear; just as Anglicans experienced radical changes a century ago, so Catholics are experiencing similar painful changes today. Indeed, Catholics are experiencing these changes at the very moment when some Anglicans are moving to Rome to avoid change. For these Anglicans, Rome represents an unchanging authority – in doctrine, in morality and in the ordination of males alone. Yet, for her, even this authority is essentially contested and contestable.

Over the last two decades, some of the most powerful theological books have been written by Roman Catholic theologians breaking away from traditional antagonisms to biblical criticism and incontestable papal teaching (chapter 8 will return to this important theological change). In liberation theology, feminist theology and hermeneutics generally, it is often Catholic theologians who lead the debate. Anne Patrick's *Liberating Conscience* follows in this radical line.

In the book she argues that Roman Catholic theology has become increasingly polarized. One section, which she terms 'fundamentalist', stresses unchanging authority and doctrine and seeks to enforce these by removing a theologian such as Professor Charles Curran from his job in a Catholic university. The other section, which she calls 'revisionist', still regards itself as orthodox and loyal to Rome, but sees change as a continuing experience of a faithful Church. Such change once involved coming to terms with a non-Jewish world; later it involved recognizing the evil of slavery; today, so she argues, it involves recognizing same-sex relationships, contraception and diverse sexual mores. At the heart of these two positions are radically different paradigms of virtue, the one 'patriarchal' and the other 'egalitarian–feminist'. The first of these paradigms, which she sees as most typical of the Bible, she depicts as follows:

A patriarchal paradigm for virtue has long dominated Catholic thinking. Its shape has been affected by the otherworldly spirituality, the theological and social patterns of domination and subordination, the misogyny, and the body-rejecting dualism characteristic of Western culture. This paradigm understands virtue to involve the control of passion by reason and the subordination of earthly values to heavenly ones. It articulates many ideals for character but tends to assume that these are appropriately assigned greater emphasis according to one's gender and social status. All Christians should be kind, chaste, just, and humble, but women are expected to excel in charity and chastity, men are trained to think in terms of justice and rights, and subordinates of both sexes are exhorted to docility and meekness.[31]

The second paradigm, which of course she espouses herself, is critical of much biblical and traditional patriarchy. She continues:

In contrast to the anthropological dualism of the patriarchal paradigm, the egalitarian–feminist paradigm understands reason itself to be embodied, and women and men to be fully equal partners in the human community. Instead of *control*, the notion of *respect* for all created reality is fundamental to this paradigm, which values the body in general and the humanity of women in particular, and promotes gender-integrated ideals for character. Rather than understanding power as control over others, this paradigm operates with a sense of power as the energy of proper relatedness. Discipline is still valued, but it is less rigidly understood. Ideals of love and justice are not segregated into separate spheres of personal and social ethics, with responsibility for realizing them assigned according to gender; instead love and justice are seen to be mutually reinforcing norms that should govern both sexes equally.[32]

My point in quoting this distinction at length is not to suggest that it cannot be criticized. On the contrary, there are many important critical questions that should be raised about how Anne Patrick establishes this second paradigm and even about the degree to which she may exaggerate the prevalence of the first. However, that is not my point here. Rather it is to illustrate that different hermeneutical perspectives can have a radical

---

[31] Patrick, *Liberating Conscience*, p. 77.
[32] Patrick, *Liberating Conscience*, pp. 78–9.

effect upon one's use and selection of distinctively Christian resources. Once this point is accepted, then the realization that modern theology offers a range of competing hermeneutical perspectives – of which Anne Patrick's egalitarian–feminism is just one – simply adds further confusion to current confusions about sexual ethics. A generation ago, bewildering choices between differing forms of historical criticism made it difficult for the theologian who took them seriously to find a reliable path through them. It was always tempting to bypass them by going back to the 'real' message of the Bible. Today hermeneutics in the form of biblical interpretation has made even this bypass problematic. None of us approaches the Bible without cultural and gender baggage. We are women or men reading Scripture, we are inhabitants of the affluent North or the poor South, we are products of particular histories, tribes and families. Biblical interpretation has shown us just how varied are our interpretations of the Bible both across cultures and across time. How then can we make reliable choices as we do theology?

Vernon Robbins, Professor of Religion at Emory University, argues in his complex book *The Tapestry of Early Christian Discourse: Rhetoric, Society and Ideology*[33] that socio-rhetorical criticism can help to give us an overview of these various historical and hermeneutical approaches to the Bible. However, in the process, he also shows just how daunting the task is. Those who study rhetoric start from oral speeches and see a constant interaction between the speaker, the speech and the audience. Speeches typically contain a mixture of repetitions, key words, narratives and differing forms of logic and emphasis, designed by the speaker to persuade the audience. Transferring these observations to written biblical texts, a socio-rhetorical approach sees them as the products of known and unknown authors addressing audiences that are often just implied in the texts and that in any case are very different from the audiences that receive them today. Like speeches, these texts also contain forms and styles that can be analysed and assessed using various literary, theological and social scientific methods. Robbins describes in detail four levels

[33] London: Routledge, 1996.

of analysis: that of the inner texture, of intertexture (texts relating to other texts and linguistic forms), of social and cultural context, and finally of ideology (texts often imply power relations within communities). For Robbins 'there is not simply a text; texts were produced by authors and they are meaningless without readers. There are not simply readers; readers are meaningless without texts to read and authors who write texts. All three presuppose historical, social, cultural and ideological relations among people and the texts they write and read.'[34]

How is a Church for the twenty-first century ever to find a convincing way through these different hermeneutical levels?

Towards a New Consensus

It would be foolish to pretend that I can wholly answer the above question. Instead, I can only point in directions that I have attempted to sketch in *Moral Leadership in a Postmodern Age*.[35] In that book, I started my own theological reconstruction with the 1995 report *The Church and Human Sexuality* produced for the Anglican Church of the Province of South Africa.[36]

This South African report begins with an extended biblical study of sexuality by the retired Rhodes University Professor of Theology, John Suggit, which seeks to identify two key biblical virtues that are held in tension on the issue of sexuality. In the process, it allows us to see that there may be abiding Christian virtues which are balanced differently in ever-changing contexts by a rich variety of Christian communities. Two sets of abiding virtues are seen as especially present in both the Old and New Testament – loving-kindness/faithfulness on the one hand and righteousness/justice on the other. God's *hesed* or loving-kindness in the Old Testament is seen as continued in the New Testament in the form of *agape* and *charis*. Suggit, schooled in the tradition of biblical theology, believes that these abiding virtues can be detected despite differing emphases between the Old Testament/Jewish Bible and the

[34] Robbins, *The Tapestry*, p. 39.
[35] Edinburgh: T&T Clark, 1997.
[36] *The Church and Human Sexuality* (Church of the Province of South Africa, 1995).

New Testament – for example, the endorsement of celibacy in the latter. A common theme between these abiding virtues is a stress upon the initiative of God's dealings with humans. The South African report sees a creative tension between this set of themes and that in both Testaments of *zedek* – that is, God's righteousness. The balance between these two sets of virtues is expressed in terms of three themes:

1. A Christian sexual ethic of love arises from faith's perception of God's ways with humankind in divine creativity and reconciliation, and in his action by which he sustains and liberates human beings so that they may live with justice (*zedek*) and integrity.
2. A sexual ethic centred in love needs to express mutual commitment between the partners, and to be liberating, enriching, honest, faithful, personally and socially responsible, life-giving and joyous.
3. Love involves an attitude towards the other partner in which the happiness and welfare of the other is of prime importance, and which is expressed in appropriate acts. In view of the frequent distortion of sexuality by abusive power both within and outside marriage, a Christian sexual ethic is committed to the liberation of sexual expression as mutual enrichment rather than as dominance and submission.[37]

The South African report sees these as abiding theological virtues in tension and then seeks to identify a number of more contingent themes. As a distinctively African report, it encourages an understanding attitude towards brideprice, customary unions and polygamy and sees them in quite a different moral light to, for example, sexual promiscuity. For the report, promiscuity 'should be seen as a misunderstanding of the meaning of sexuality and a hindrance to the development of full human personality. . . as being opposed to God's will for human beings'.[38]

In terms of my theological analysis, the chief merit of this South African report is that it distinguishes carefully between,

---

[37] *The Church and Human Sexuality*, para. B4.
[38] *The Church and Human Sexuality*, para. E6.

on the one hand, abiding Christian/Jewish virtues that are held in tension in the Bible and in subsequent Christian history, and, on the other, contingent contexts and recipients that are constantly changing. By identifying at the outset a set of relevant theological virtues, it is then able to bring them to the various moral issues surrounding sexuality and changing patterns of family life. An abiding pattern is faithful and loving monogamy, which is seen as the Christian ideal both for sexuality in general and for the responsible upbringing of children. In this analysis, customary marriage and polygamy, in the context of African society, are seen as less than the ideal rather than inherently opposed to it.

Vernon Robbins' socio-rhetorical criticism acts as an important reminder that, in Christian ethics, author, text and audience constantly interact with each other, changing over time and across time within Christian communities. We change, our context changes and our perception of the Bible changes. If this had not been the case, then Christianity would soon have become moribund and anachronistic. Nevertheless we are spared from pure relativism, becoming in the process little more than echoes of our surrounding societies, by our constant interactions with Christian texts, especially in a context of Christian worship. It is thus important to distinguish carefully between the abiding and the contingent, perhaps as follows:

Way 1: Faithful and righteous family life, based upon love and mutuality, remains an *abiding Christian ideal for all societies*. It is not, of course, the only ideal, since in the New Testament, as well as in much of subsequent Christian history, dedicated celibacy is also an ideal – although, by definition, not a sexual ideal. There has also been a long-standing recognition in Christian ethics that family life can be distorted, either by unfaithfulness or by unrighteousness.

Way 2: Some forms of sexuality, which are sadly present in many societies, are *inherently opposed to this ideal and are thus sinful* – for example, promiscuity (both heterosexual and homosexual), adultery, prostitution, child pornography, active paedophilia, and sadomasochism. From a Christian perspective, they remain deeply sinful, however much some elements of secular society seek to justify them.

Likewise, families which are deeply distorted by unfaithfulness and/or unrighteousness can become inherently opposed to the Christian ideal. Monogamy as such is not a guarantee against such distortion.

Way 3: There are other forms of behaviour which, in terms of Christian virtues, are not inherently sinful but which are still less than ideal. That is to say, they *share some of the Christian virtues without exemplifying them all.* This group contains both patterns which are present 'in nature', such as childlessness through spontaneous sterility, and others, such as faithful cohabitation, which are products more of changing cultures. Faithful homosexual relationships may belong either to nature or to culture (morally that may not be too important since a homosexual orientation is not something an individual chooses).

The last way allows for considerable differences amongst those of us who try to be and hope to be faithful Christians. Yet if the model that Vernon Robbins offers is accepted, then perhaps the Church in the twenty-first century will learn to see these differences as a sign of a vivacious and dynamic Church (as will be evident from the previous chapter, the 1998 Lambeth Conference did not of course share this vision). Christian virtues in tension abide but our application and interpretation of these virtues constantly change. That, I believe, has always been the reality of a living Church, especially a Church set within *Changing Worlds*.

PART TWO

Changing Patterns of Churchgoing

5

Churchgoing Decline – A Case-study

The first four chapters of this book are all concerned with changing moral perceptions and their implications both for churches and for society at large. This and the following two chapters turn instead to changing patterns of churchgoing and the challenges that they present to churches in *changing worlds*. My own research over the last two decades has been almost equally divided between these two areas.

This second part of *Changing Worlds* starts with a case-study, namely Kent, that sets the scene for the two chapters that follow. Starting with this case-study, a picture begins to emerge that can be set into a broader context in the next chapter. The focus in both of these chapters is upon churchgoing. Of course there are many more elusive ways in which individuals may express their religious beliefs and feelings. Yet, in the sociology of religion the study of implicit, unofficial or 'folk' religion (there is no agreement here about labels), while widely recognized as important, is also sadly elusive.[1] Chapter 7 then considers three further case-studies to see whether or not the sort of churchgoing decline evident in chapters 5 and 6 is an inevitable feature of modernity.

Expressed bluntly, throughout the twentieth century Kent, like other parts of Britain, has seen a sharp decline in churchgoing. This decline has not been spread evenly over all denominations and there are distinctive features to the overall pattern in Kent. Nevertheless, decline in regular churchgoing, and indeed in most other visible forms of participation in religious organizations in Kent, has been a dominant feature.

---

[1] See P.H. Vrijhof and J. Waardenburg, *Official and Popular Religion: Analysis of a Theme for Religious Studies*, (Netherlands: Mouton, 1979); Edward Bailey (ed.), *A Workshop in Popular Religion* (Partners Publication, 1996); and Edward Bailey, 'Implicit Religion: A Bibliographical Introduction', *Social Compass* 37 (1990), pp. 499–509.

Unlike London, the relative absence of ethnic minorities means that there is little evidence in Kent of any compensating participation in non-Christian religious organizations. In contrast, tourist visits to churches, and especially to Canterbury Cathedral, have shown an increasing popularity. There are now almost as many visitors to this Cathedral[2] as there are attendances put together in all of the other Kent Anglican churches in the course of a year.

Bromley Churchgoing – Case-study

Obtaining accurate figures for regular churchgoing across denominations that cover Kent (or any other county) for the whole of the twentieth century is probably impossible. The Church of England has kept average Sunday attendance figures[3] only since 1968 and few other denominations have recorded such figures for even that length of time. MARC Europe censuses[4] across denominations were made only in 1979, 1989 and 1998. The only other comparable data are from the nineteenth rather than the twentieth century, namely the 1851 Religious Census.[5]

Bromley, however, is an exception. Fortunately R. Mudie-Smith's invaluable census of London churches[6] in 1903

[2] Approximately two million.

[3] All Church of England national statistics, unless otherwise stated, are taken from annual *Church Statistics: Some Facts and Figures About the Church of England* (London: Central Board of Finance of the Church of England, Church House).

[4] These are mostly contained in Peter Brierley (ed.), *Prospects for the Nineties: Trends and Tables From the 1989 English Church Census* (MARC Europe, 1991). Some information has also been taken from his *Prospects for the Eighties: From a Census of the Churches in 1979* (London: Bible Society, 1980). Where 1979 figures were revised in 1991 the latter have been used. *The English Church Attendance Survey 1998* reported in Peter Brierley (ed.), *UK Christian Handbook: Religious Trends 2000/20001 No.2* (London: Christian Research and Harper Collins), is used for national and regional trends but did not itemize Kent separately.

[5] Horace Mann (ed.), *1851 Census Great Britain: Report and Tables on Religious Worship England and Wales* (British Parliamentary Papers, Population 10, 1852–3, reprinted by Irish University Press, Shannon, 1970).

[6] Richard Mudie-Smith (ed.), *The Religious Life of London* (London: Hodder, 1904).

extended just as far as Bromley. As a result, it is possible to make some useful comparisons in this area of solid middle-class, suburban Kent churchgoing. Unfortunately there are some caveats to make. The census of Bromley churches on 11 October 1903 was made on a wet day. It was also a census made by enumerators standing outside church doors rather than by asking ministers and church officials to make estimates.[7] And, crucially, it largely ignored Sunday school attendances. These factors may well have suppressed the figures in 1903 compared with 1851 or 1993. This makes it difficult to know the exact change between 1851 and 1903, but it cannot disguise, even if it may underestimate, the manifest decline between 1903 and 1993.

In 1851, morning and evening attendances combined (including Sunday school) across denominations in Bromley[8] amounted to 40.6 per cent of the local population. This population rose from 17,637 in 1851 to 27,292 in 1903. Morning and evening attendances combined (but not including Sunday school) by 1903 amounted to 37.9 per cent. The addition of Sunday school figures for 1903 is likely to have taken these attendances at least to the level of 1851. Of course, some of those attending in the morning may have attended again in the evening (the 1903 census estimates that in Greater London 36 per cent of morning attenders went again in the evening) so attendances cannot be equated with attenders. However, if morning attendances alone are taken, then at least the very minimum numbers of attenders can be established. On this basis, 28.8 per cent of the population were present in Bromley churches and chapels in 1851 but only 19.0 per cent in 1903 (although, once again, the first figure includes Sunday school and the second does not). As happened elsewhere in the country,[9] two factors contributed to this apparent decline: a sharp decline in Church of England morning attendances (from 21.5 per cent to 10.6 per cent) and an increase, perhaps

---

[7] For the effects of weather and census method see Table 8 of my *The Myth of the Empty Church* (London: SPCK, 1993).

[8] Proportionate estimates have been included in these calculations for four Anglican churches and one independent church missing from the original returns.

[9] See *The Myth of the Empty Church*, ch. 6.

resulting from the introduction of street lighting, in overall evening attendances (from 11.8 per cent to 18.8 per cent).

Compared with most other urban areas, Bromley was evidently a place of fairly high churchgoing in 1903. It will be seen in the next chapter that inner Greater London and Liverpool both had lower levels of churchgoing by this date. Eight[10] large towns had average combined morning and evening attendances then of 26.6 per cent, compared with Bromley's 37.9 per cent. In Greater London, the only times attendances were substantially higher was when there was no rain.[11]

The population of Bromley[12] rose again by 1993, reaching 44,146. However, churchgoing declined sharply in both proportional and absolute terms. The relative absence of evening services in many churches today makes it more difficult to compare churchgoing on the same basis as 1851/1903. In addition, attendance figures in many denominations are collected only on the basis of separate attenders rather than attendances. However, using the 1903 estimate of Greater London 'twicers', it is possible to produce some broad comparisons. Keeping in mind the three factors of weather, enumeration and Sunday schools, on this basis 31 per cent of the Bromley population were in church in 1903 but only 10.5 per cent by 1993. Thus a threefold decline, and perhaps in reality a fourfold decline, seems to have taken place in these ninety years. Or, to express this differently, there were some 8,472 attenders on that Sunday in 1903 but only 4,631 on an average Sunday in 1993 despite a greatly increased population.

Stated so baldly these figures disguise some more subtle changes between denominations in Bromley during the twentieth century. The Roman Catholic Church has increased

---

[10] See *The Myth of the Empty Church*, Table 16. The eight towns were: Chester, Hull, Lincoln, Middlesbrough, Wallasey, Whitehaven, Workington and York.

[11] See *The Myth of the Empty Church*, pp. 174ff. High Barnet (60 per cent), Ealing (51 per cent) and Woodford (50 per cent) all had remarkably high attendances in fine weather in 1903.

[12] As defined in the 1903 survey by the Anglican parishes of St Peter and St Paul, St Mark, St John, Holy Trinity, St George, Christ Church and St Mary. I am most grateful to the Rev. Richard Freedman for supplying me with their population figures.

both proportionately and absolutely, whereas the United Reformed Church has literally been decimated. Anglicans and Methodists have both declined sharply, whereas Baptists have increased in absolute but not in proportionate terms. The Salvation Army now has one of its strongest congregations in Greater London at Bromley. There is also considerable fluidity between House Churches and the evangelical congregations of the Baptists and the Anglicans. So, although Bromley church-going during this century is down by at least two-thirds, relative balances between denominations are still shifting.

The Anglican churches also suggest that balances are still shifting within denominations. In 1903 the 4,620 estimated attenders represented 16.9 per cent of the Bromley population. The 1,312 attenders in 1993 represented just 3 per cent. This 3 per cent is still higher than the 2.6 per cent for the Rochester Diocese as a whole and higher still than the 1993 national 2.2 per cent (although nothing like the 4.2 per cent for the more rural Hereford Diocese). In 1903 the Parish Church of St Peter and St Paul had congregations more than twice the size of most other local churches (619 in the morning and 898 in the evening), St Luke's Church had the next largest congregations and Christ Church the smallest (80 morning and 67 evening). By 1993 the Parish Church remained strong, but the evangelical Christ Church was now the strongest and St Luke's the weakest.

In 1903 there was a single Roman Catholic church in Bromley with 177 attenders (0.6 per cent of the population), whereas by 1993 there were two churches with a combined 1,450 attenders (3.3 per cent of the population). Catholics in Bromley, but not in Kent as a whole, are now the most numerous regular worshippers. St Joseph's Church today has six masses each Sunday, drawing people from a wide radius. Two Catholic churches serve the same area as and slightly more worshippers than eight Anglican churches. Not surprisingly, all the Anglican churches, except Christ Church and St Peter and St Paul's, appear thinly attended in comparison. Ironically, in 1903 it was only Christ Church that had a thinner congregation than St Joseph's.

Baptists in Bromley have shown remarkable resilience in the twentieth century. In 1903 they had four churches with an estimate of 748 attenders. By 1993 there were five Baptist

churches in Bromley (one of them Strict Baptist) with a total of
926 attenders. The earlier figure represented 2.7 per cent
of the local population and the later 2.1 per cent. The central
Baptist Church today has much the largest congregations, with
350 adults and 70 children typically present in the morning and
200 adults in the evening (half of the latter having already
attended in the morning). It is hardly surprising that some of
the smaller evangelical congregations felt the draft both from
this congregation and from that at Christ Church. One chapel,
currently with an attendance of just fifteen adults, reported that
until a few years ago it had a congregation of one hundred
which has now been largely 'fed' to other churches.
Churchgoers with young children not surprisingly find the
central Baptist Church more appealing than this thinly
attended chapel with an entirely adult congregation. As
happened at the turn of the century in some towns when the
Salvation Army became popular at the expense of local Baptists,
and in the previous century when Primitive Methodists
benefited from defecting Wesleyan Methodists, so in the 1990s
a similar process apparently continues in Bromley. This time
around, such transfers benefit the Baptists.

Finally, Bromley Methodists, Congregationalists and
Presbyterians have all experienced severe decline. In 1903
there were five Methodist chapels and missions with an
estimated 1,244 attenders, representing 4.6 per cent of the
Bromley population. By 1993 there were three chapels, but now
with only 245 attenders, representing 0.6 per cent of the local
population. Congregationalists and Presbyterians, each now a
part of the United Reformed Church though retaining their
own church building, had congregations representing 4.0 per
cent of the local population in 1903. Ninety years later, their
two congregations represented just 0.4 per cent. Like most of
the Anglican churches, they have found it difficult to recruit
new members in an area with an array of active Baptist and
evangelical churches. Alongside these established Free
Churches, there is also a small Society of Friends. It, too, makes
little numerical impact upon local churchgoing.

The institutional weakness of many of the churches in
Bromley today is underlined by the relative absence of children
within them. In the Anglican churches, only 252 children were
recorded as usually attending Sunday services in 1993. In

contrast, in 1903 there were 878 children present in the morning service alone. At that time, at least twice that number of children might be expected to attend Sunday school in the afternoon (the census recorded such attendances only in Chelsea). It seems likely, then, that the rate of decline in attendance is higher within these churches amongst children than amongst adults. In Rowntree's surveys of churchgoing in York,[13] a relative absence of children proved to be a dangerous indicator for churches. Poor attendances amongst children bodes ill for churches in the future.[14] Even in the Catholic Church in Bromley, attendances of young people are little better. Within the Methodist and United Reformed Church, attendances of young people are considerably worse.

Bromley is still an area of relatively high churchgoing. It also differs from the county as a whole in a number of respects. In the county of Kent, there has been an Anglican dominance throughout the twentieth century. In Bromley, the strong presence of Roman Catholics, who are comparatively few elsewhere in Kent, and of Baptists curtails this dominance. However, in other respects Bromley and Kent as a whole are similar. Both have an array of small independent congregations, without having strong ethnic minorities. In both, there is evidence of fluidity amongst these independent congregations. Each of these factors needs to be considered separately.

Anglican Dominance in Kent

In 1851, Kent was still a predominantly Anglican county with Anglicans representing 62.7 per cent of all attendances (in contrast to a national figure of only 52.1 per cent). By 1989 this balance had changed somewhat, yet with Anglicans in Kent still representing 45.0 per cent of attenders, in contrast to a national figure of 30.1 per cent and a London figure of just 16.7 per cent.

---

[13] B. Seebohm Rowntree, *Poverty: A Study of Town Life* (London: Macmillan, 1901), *Poverty and Progress: A Second Social Study of York* (London: Longmans/Green, 1941) and *English Life and Leisure: A Social Study* (London: Longmans/Green, 1951); written with G. R. Lavers.

[14] See *The Myth of the Empty Church*, ch. 8.

Even in 1851, Anglican dominance was uneven. As sometimes happened elsewhere, the Cathedral City of Canterbury had some very strong Free Church congregations. Anglican attendances there amounted only to 50.9 per cent of all attendances. Thirteen Anglican churches shared these attendances, with mean attendances of 140 in the morning and 98 in the evening. In contrast, the Wesleyan Methodist Church in Canterbury had a morning congregation of 510 and an evening congregation of 828 and the Independent Church there had congregations of 537 and 600 respectively. Even the Lady Huntingdon Connexion Chapel had congregations of 280 and 220. Clearly, the citizens of Canterbury were not overawed by the Church of England.

In deeply rural parts of Kent Anglican dominance in 1851 was more apparent. For example, on the Romney Marsh 69.0 per cent of all attendances were Anglican and afternoon attendances in Anglican churches there amounted to a remarkable 31.2 per cent of the population. Thirteen of the twenty churches on the Marsh were Anglican, five small chapels were Wesleyan Methodist and two Baptist. Mean attendances at the Anglican churches were 66 in the morning and 131 in the afternoon. Wesleyans had 34 in the morning, 63 in the afternoon and 99 in the evening. Baptists had only 15 in the morning, 17 in the afternoon and 53 in the evening. Since there were no evening services in the Anglican churches, it is possible that here, as elsewhere in rural areas,[15] some of the population went to an Anglican church in the morning or afternoon and to a Wesleyan or Baptist chapel in the evening. At the end of the twentieth century, many deeply rural areas are experiencing a rather different form of ecumenism. Free Churches are increasingly withdrawing from rural areas altogether, leaving those who still go to church with little option but to attend an Anglican church. Anglicans, in turn, in areas such as the Romney Marsh, cluster ever larger groups of churches together into a single charge.

In 1968 there was still a clear difference between the more rural Canterbury Diocese and the Rochester Diocese. Both had

---

[15] cf. James Obelkevich, *Religion and Rural Society: South Lindsey 1825–1875* (Oxford: Oxford University Press, 1976).

levels of attendance above the national mean of 3.5 per cent. In the case of Rochester, attendance at 3.7 per cent was only slightly higher than this mean but in Canterbury it was distinctly higher at 4.5 per cent. To set these figures into context, the most rural diocese, Hereford, had an attendance of 6.5 per cent, in Bath and Wells it was 6.4 per cent and in Exeter 6.0 per cent. London and Birmingham, in contrast, had only 2.1 per cent. Another clear indicator of rural/urban differences is Easter communicants. In Hereford in 1968 these amounted to 13.4 per cent of the population aged over fourteen, in Bath and Wells 10.8 per cent and in Exeter 10.2 per cent. However, in London they were 2.8 per cent and in Birmingham only 2.7 per cent. Thus a rural area might expect twice as many communicants as usual at Easter, whereas an urban area might expect less than a third more. Canterbury, with Easter communicants at 6.8 per cent, was still clearly different from Rochester at 5.1 per cent. However, by 1993 these differences had narrowed. With a national rate of usual attendance of 2.2 per cent, both dioceses now recorded 2.6 per cent. Easter communicants had also fallen to 4.0 per cent in Canterbury and to 3.4 per cent in Rochester, compared with a national rate of 3.3 per cent.

The indication here that the Canterbury Diocese is declining faster than the Rochester Diocese is confirmed by electoral roll statistics. In 1962 these amounted to 76,400 for Canterbury and 68,200 for Rochester. By 1973 both figures had declined drastically, but now it was Rochester which had the higher figure of 50,068 and Canterbury only 48,154. After the transfer of the Croydon Deanery from Canterbury Diocese to Southwark, the Canterbury electoral roll figure dropped further to 23,700 in 1988, with Rochester declining only to 39,300. Both dioceses have also seen a radical decline in infant baptisms, although in this instance Rochester has declined slightly faster than Canterbury. In 1968 Canterbury's baptism rate per one hundred live births was 53.4 and Rochester 53.2; by 1994 this had declined to 30.4 and 24.1 respectively.

Another area that shows a sharp decline, especially in the Canterbury Diocese, is the number of stipendiary parochial clergy. In 1933 there were 403 stipendiary clergy in the Canterbury Diocese: this declined to 307 by 1963, and to 179 by 1994. Some allowance must be made in the final figure for the transfer of the Croydon Deanery, but it is clear that the overall number has virtually halved over the six decades. In Rochester there has also been a decline, but it has not been so dramatic: moving from 296 in 1933, to 277 by 1963, and to 226 by 1995. Lying behind these different rates of decline are shifting concepts of viable livings. In 1963 in Canterbury, 26.4 per cent of incumbents were in livings of less than a thousand people: in Rochester it was only 15.5 per cent. Not surprisingly, Canterbury's 179 stipendiary clergy now have 329 churches to look after, whereas the 226 clergy in Rochester have 264 churches. The problems facing the Canterbury clergy are not as difficult in this respect as those facing the 121 Hereford clergy looking after 425 churches, yet they are problems that are likely to increase over the years ahead.

However, there is one important area that does show a steady increase, namely weekly giving in church collections. If such giving is measured per electoral roll member (a measure which, of course, favours Canterbury), then it has increased from 2s 5d for Canterbury and 2s 9d for Rochester in 1962, to £1.75 and £1.72 in 1988, and to £4.30 and £4.11 in 1994. Thus, even before the results of the unwise investment policies of the Church Commissioners became widely known, weekly giving had risen significantly in Kent parishes. Indeed, the rise in Kent has been faster than the national mean of 2s 7d for 1962, £1.45 for 1988, and £3.42 for 1994.

Relative Absence of Roman Catholics in Kent

Another distinctive feature of religion in Kent is the relative absence of Roman Catholics. Bromley is sufficiently near to London, which (as will be seen in the next chapter) has for long had a higher concentration of Catholics. In other parts of Kent there are surprisingly few Roman Catholics. This appears to be a phenomenon with a long history.

In the *Recusant Returns* of 1676, only 0.2 per cent of the population of Kent was returned as 'Papist'. Nationally the figure was 0.5 per cent and in London it was 0.7 per cent. In the 1851 Religious Census, only 1.4 per cent of attendances in Kent were by Catholics, whereas in the country as a whole it was 3.5 per cent and in London 6.6 per cent. Kent in 1851 had only thirteen Roman Catholic churches, largely in the north of the county. In the MARC Europe Survey of 1989, Catholic attenders amounted to 18.5 per cent in Kent, compared to a national figure of 34.8 per cent and to a London figure of 39.2 per cent. By 1989 there were 129 Catholic churches in Kent. Of course there are caveats to be made about each of these sets of figures. For example, the 1851 Religious Census tended to underestimate attendances at multiple morning masses.[16] And even today, estimates of congregation sizes are often given to outside researchers in very 'round' numbers. Nevertheless, they suggest a consistent overall pattern.

Indeed, the comparatively small Catholic presence in Kent makes overall churchgoing rates appear rather small. So, in the 1989 MARC Europe Survey, Kent had an adult attendance rate of 8.0 per cent, whereas the national figure was 9.5 per cent simply because in Kent only 1.6 per cent of the adult population attended a Catholic church but nationally it was 3.4 per cent. Even the average size of Catholic adult attendances per church in Kent, namely 162, is rather small compared with the national mean of 355. Nevertheless, Catholic attenders in Kent (and elsewhere in the country as the next chapter will show) do seem to be declining. MARC Europe suggests that Catholic adult attenders in Kent as a whole have declined from 2.4 per cent of the adult population in 1979 to the 1.6 per cent of 1989 and, more speculatively, that in the course of fifteen years from 1975, attenders declined by a third from 29,400 to 19,500.

Changing Balances Between Other Denominations in Kent

Changing balances between the smaller Christian denominations in Bromley have already been noted. A comparison between the 1851 Census and the 1989 Survey helps to put these changes into a broader map of Kent. It is always risky to make projections for the future, but some speculations will also be attempted.

As in Bromley so in Kent as a whole, it is the Methodist and United Reformed Churches that have declined fastest relative

---

[16] See *The Myth of the Empty Church*, ch. 6.

to other Free Churches. In 1851, Methodist attendances at all services in Kent (that is, including afternoon services) amounted to 14.2 per cent of all denominational attendances. By 1989 Methodist attenders in Kent represented just 6.9 per cent of all attenders. Thus, at the two ends of a period when all denominations, except the Catholic Church, drastically declined overall, Methodists declined at twice that rate. Congregationalists and Presbyterians, who eventually constituted the United Reformed Church, declined at three times the rate. In 1851, Presbyterian attendances represented 0.5 per cent of all attendances and Independents/Congregationalists 9.2 per cent. By 1989, United Reformed Church attenders represented only 3.2 per cent of all attenders. The somewhat speculative 1975 figures recorded by MARC Europe suggest that the combined Methodist and United Reformed Church adult attenders declined from some 11,000 then to 9,400 in 1989. Less speculatively, by 1989 the mean attendance for each congregation was only 65 adults and 20 children. Thus, individual congregations typically appeared thin and the proportion of children (24 per cent) was considerably less than that recorded in 1903 at Chelsea (43 per cent). If similar losses are sustained uniformly in the next century, neither denomination may survive in Kent much beyond the mid-point. More likely, perhaps, is that a small minority of congregations may survive, and even thrive, but the majority (especially in rural areas) will disappear. In either event, it will be difficult in the twenty-first century for these denominations to match their presence in the nineteenth century.

In contrast, Baptists in Kent, although sharing in the general decline of other denominations, have maintained their relative position well. In 1851, Baptist attendances amounted to 9.4 per cent of all denominational attendances: by 1989 they still had 9.7 per cent of all attenders. The latter is about twice their national rate, but still represents only 0.8 per cent of the population of Kent. In 1989 they had a slightly higher proportion of children (27 per cent) than the Methodist or United Reformed Church, and their mean attendance for each congregation was 88 adults and 33 children. Nevertheless, MARC Europe suggests that even they declined from 10,300 attenders in 1979 to 9,700 in 1989 and, more crucially, child attenders declined from 4,500 in 1985 to 3,600 in 1989.

However, these figures probably have to be set alongside those categorized by MARC Europe in 1989 as 'independents'. The survey records an increase of children in this category from 5,200 in 1985 to 6,500 in 1989 and of adults from 5,400 in 1979 to a remarkable 10,600 in 1989.

Some of these latter figures do need to be treated with considerable caution, since the 1979 survey of smaller denominations contains many estimates. Nevertheless, as in Bromley, they do suggest a situation of some considerable fluidity in these denominations. Figures for adult Pentecostals in Kent, dropping from 4,400 in 1979 to 2,800 in 1989, are certainly in line with this fluidity. But will the growth, if accurate, of independent churches be sustained into the twenty-first century? MARC Europe in 1991 projected a continuing decline in the Catholic Church, United Reformed Church, Methodist Church and Church of England. The results of *The English Church Attendance Survey* 1998 did seem to confirm this projection, as will be seen in the next chapter. The MARC Europe 1991 projection for the new independent churches was for a considerable increase – although not an increase that will actually offset the overall decline caused by the other denominations (the 1998 survey modifies this projection by observing an increase in 'new' rather than 'independent' churches). My own assessment elsewhere[17] is more cautious. Looking at national data over a sufficient time-span, there is a long-established pattern of short-term growth in newer/smaller denominations. On the other hand, taking a single fixed point, in Kent in 1989 it was the independent churches that apparently had the highest rate of children present (38 per cent), a higher rate even than their national rate (31 per cent). If that can be sustained into the twenty-first century, it would augur well for their survival in Kent.

Finally, Kent has no strong visible presence of non-Christian religions. In 1851, Jewish attendances at synagogues in Kent represented 0.1 per cent of all church attendances, whereas in London they represented 0.3 per cent. Even today it is difficult for an Orthodox Jew to live in East Kent. Within the University of Kent at Canterbury some Orthodox Jews choose instead to

---

[17] In *The Myth of the Empty Church*, pp. 218ff.

live near a synagogue in London or Rochester, since there is no longer one in Canterbury itself (the synagogue there had just 53 seats which were only half full in 1851). Some 400 Muslim students and Muslims spread more widely in East Kent have their own service every Friday in the University. Whereas the followers of almost any faith can find a place of worship in London, choice is much more restricted in Kent. Even the attempt to build a Multi-Faith Centre in the University finally faltered in 1996 through lack of general support.

This chapter has, as stated at the outset, focused upon the visible features of religious institutions in Kent in the twentieth century. Of course, the generally bleak picture that emerges from this says nothing about the spiritual vitality and commitment of religious institutions, their members, or of the wider public beyond them. But does it represent changes that are happening in the rest of Britain? And if it does, how are these changes to be understood? The next two chapters will wrestle with these questions.

6

Responses to Churchgoing Decline

On face value, the previous chapter points to evidence of considerable decline within British churches during the twentieth century. Bromley is, after all, an affluent area of middle-class suburbia with some well-attended Baptist, Anglican and Roman Catholic churches. If there is likely to be any area in England of comparatively flourishing churchgoing today then Bromley is an obvious choice. Yet between 1903 and 1993 this prime location for institutional churches appears to have experienced at least a threefold and, more likely, a fourfold overall decline in churchgoing. It is evidence such as this that has persuaded most sociologists of religion today that (whatever the reasons behind it or its wider implications) institutional Christianity in Britain is undergoing considerable decline. In contrast, the official position taken within a number of denominations is that such evidence is deeply misleading. Officials within the Church of England, in particular, have become increasingly suspicious of supposed statistics of decline and have made considerable efforts to produce counter evidence. The contrast between sociologists (some of whom are themselves members of churches) and church officials is fascinating for a study of *changing worlds*.

Sociologists and Church Decline

The last four decades have seen deep divisions among sociologists of religion on the issue of 'secularization'. Among British sociologists of religion, the fundamental differences between Bryan Wilson and David Martin in the 1960s are still mirrored today by the differences, for example, between Steve Bruce and

Grace Davie. I have mapped out these differences elsewhere,[1] so here I will focus more specifically upon certain features of this debate.

Bryan Wilson's seminal analysis made at length in his 1960s book *Religion in Secular Society*,[2] when compared with recent studies in the sociology of religion, shows both how the debate about secularization has changed over the years and just how resistant senior parts of the Church of England are to some forms of sociological analysis. More to the point, there is evidence that parts of the Church of England (perhaps like Churches elsewhere) are capable of very selective reading when confronted with distressing 'evidence'.

Wilson depicted secularization quite simply as 'the process whereby religious thinking, practice and institutions lose social significance'.[3] In his early writing, the 'process' here seemed to be an ineluctable process deriving from modernity. Most secularization theorists today tend, in contrast, to be agnostic about whether or not this is an ineluctable process.[4] However, Wilson's three elements of secularization – namely, that it involves religious thinking, practice and institutions – remain crucial to many recent accounts. Wilson argued that in the past (and still today, in less modernized societies) all three were at the centre of society, whereas throughout the Western world today they are not:

> In the twentieth century that situation has manifestly changed, and the process of change continues. But change does not occur evenly, nor in necessarily similar ways in different societies. Religious *practice* may atrophy, as it has, for example, in Scandinavian countries; or it may persist in its traditional forms (and even become more extensive) whilst its social and cultural meaning changes, as in the United States. Religious *institutions* may also continue to show, as in America, remarkable resilience, but they may do so by

---

[1] In *Churchgoing and Christian Ethics* (Cambridge: Cambridge University Press, 1999), ch. 3.

[2] London: C. A. Watts, 1966.

[3] Wilson, *Religion in Secular Society*, p. 14.

[4] See Steve Bruce, *Religion in the Modern World* (Oxford: Oxford University Press, 1996).

transforming themselves from largely traditional styles to organisations which embody all the rational bureaucratic authority assumptions of other, non-religious, organisations in advanced society. Religious *thinking* is perhaps the area which evidences most conspicuous change. Men act less and less in response to religious motivation: they assess the world in empirical and rational terms, and find themselves involved in rational organisations and rationally determined roles which allow small scope for such religious predilections as they might privately entertain.[5]

I argued at the time that this depiction of secularization is not without problems.[6] For example, Wilson claimed here that both low churchgoing in Britain and high churchgoing in the United States lacked social significance and were therefore equally evidence of secularization. So, presumably, it was irrelevant whether churchgoing was low or high; what was important was simply its social significance. Yet within a few pages, Wilson was rehearsing declining statistics within the Church of England precisely because it was evidence of secularization. Furthermore, the statistics that he quoted covered a fairly limited time scale and ignored those in other churches (despite making broader claims about Britain as a whole).

Criteria about 'social significance' in this area remain elusive today. However, British data about the extent of the decline of institutional religious practice and belief have become much more firmly based among sociologists of religion. In this more limited respect, Wilson's instincts have been confirmed a generation later. There is now overwhelming evidence that, whatever more privatized and less conventional forms of religious practice may or may not still flourish in Britain (which can seldom be measured diachronically), most forms of religious practice sponsored by institutional churches have declined throughout the twentieth century. There is also now convincing evidence that central Christian beliefs upheld by most churches are held by fewer and fewer British people.

---

[5] Wilson, *Religion in Secular Society*, p. 10.
[6] See my *The Social Context of Theology* (Oxford: Mowbray, 1975), pp. 94ff.

To illustrate this point of convergence among sociologists of religion it is worth mentioning two recent works in particular, Grace Davie's *Religion in Modern Europe: A Memory Mutates*[7] and Callum Brown's *The Death of Christian Britain*.[8] What is remarkable about both of these works is that Davie and Brown were two of the leading British critics of secularization theories. Davie remains a critic but now unambiguously admits institutional decline, whereas Brown has become a strong proponent of secularization theory and sees institutional decline as clear evidence of de-Christianization since the 1960s.

Davie summarizes the empirical findings made in the 1980s and 1990s of the influential European Value Systems Study Group as follows:

> There are, broadly speaking, five religious indicators within the data: denominational allegiance, reported church attendance, attitudes towards the church, indicators of religious belief, and some measurement of subjective religious disposition ... What emerges ... is a clustering of two types of variable: on the one hand, those concerned with feelings, experience, and the more numinous religious beliefs; on the other, those which measure religious orthodoxy, ritual participation, and institutional attachment. It is, moreover, the latter (the more orthodox indicators of religious attachment) which display, most obviously, an undeniable degree of secularization throughout Western Europe. In contrast, the former (the less institutional indicators) demonstrate considerable persistence in some aspects of religious life.[9]

Brown goes much further than this. He states his new thesis dramatically at the outset:

> This book is about the death of Christian Britain – the demise of the nation's core religious and moral identity. As historical changes go, this has been no lingering and drawn-out affair. It took several centuries (in what historians used to call the Dark Ages) to convert Britain to Christianity, but it has taken less than forty years for the country to forsake it.

---

[7] Oxford: Oxford University Press, 2000.
[8] London: Routledge, 2001.
[9] Davie, *Religion in Modern Europe*, p. 7.

For a thousand years, Christianity penetrated deeply into the lives of the people, enduring Reformation, Enlightenment and industrial revolution by adapting to each new social and cultural context that arose. Then, really quite suddenly in 1963, something very profound ruptured the character of the nation and its people, sending organised Christianity on a downward spiral to the margins of social significance. In unprecedented numbers, the British people since the 1960s have stopped going to church, have allowed their church membership to lapse, have stopped marrying in church and have neglected to baptise their children. Meanwhile, their children, the two generations who grew to maturity in the last thirty years of the twentieth century, stopped going to Sunday school, stopped entering confirmation or communicant classes, and rarely, if ever, stepped inside a church to worship in their entire lives. The cycle of inter-generational renewal of Christian affiliation, a cycle which had for so many centuries tied the people however closely or loosely to the churches and to Christian moral benchmarks, was permanently disrupted in the 'swinging sixties'. Since then, a formerly religious people have entirely forsaken organised Christianity in a sudden plunge into a truly secular condition.[10]

There are some obvious differences between these two quotations. Brown is convinced that this evidence of church decline does indicate 'a sudden plunge into a truly secular condition', whereas Davie manifestly does not. For Brown, de-Christianization and secularization are one and the same phenomenon, whereas for Davie they are not. Brown's thesis is specifically related to a radical change in culture effected by the so-called 'swinging sixties' and the extensive evidence that he offers (consisting of both church statistics and oral history data) focuses very specifically upon Britain, albeit making wider claims about the West, whereas Davie's focus is upon Europe in all its varied complexities. Nevertheless, both of these once staunch critics of secularization theorists do detect clear evidence of declining Christian practices and beliefs. Yet,

[10] Brown, *The Death of Christian Britain*, p. 1.

ironically, it is this evidence that a number of officials within British churches are anxious to deny.

José Casanova's influential *Public Religions in the Modern World*[11] represents a position somewhere between Brown and Davie. However, like Davie, he is less convinced than Wilson that modernity necessarily brings about secularization. Or, more accurately, he believes that only some features of secularization accompany modernity. For example, he does not follow Wilson in believing that only privatized forms of religion that lack social or political significance can survive in the modern world. *Public Religions in the Modern World* supplies some startling examples of the opposite – namely public forms of religion that are still surprisingly influential in modern societies. These diverge sharply from Wilson's assessment in the final sentence of the quotation above (and, of course, from Brown). For Casanova, religious resurgence, sometimes in fundamentalist forms but at other times not, is as much a feature of the modern world as is religious decline. Nevertheless, there is one facet of secularization that he does consider to be ubiquitous in the modern world, namely a process of separation or differentiation of Church and state. He argues that this has happened or will eventually happen everywhere in the modern world. This claim has obvious implications for an established Church like the Church of England. Indeed, Casanova argues that visible institutional religious decline has been fastest in those countries that have resisted disestablishment. Like Wilson he points particularly at Scandinavia, but Britain could also be a prime candidate.

Long-term Religious Decline

The trouble is that evidence of long-term decline in formal religious participation in Britain is overwhelming. Wherever overall participation rates can be compared longitudinally over the last one hundred years, they typically show this decline – across Christian denominations and even allowing for some recent growth in Eastern religious traditions there. The

[11] Chicago: University of Chicago Press, 1994.

twentieth century saw a sharp and continuous decline, albeit with some denominational variations, in active support for both Christian churches and Jewish synagogues in Britain, without any clear indication that this decline has yet halted at the beginning of the twenty-first century. Indeed, and in contrast to the Brown thesis, this decline predates 1963 by almost one hundred years. There are technical problems in collecting comparable data to map this decline in a linear fashion. However, when like is carefully compared with like (as the previous chapter has already done with Bromley and Kent) within most denominations and from one area to the next, the extent of this decline becomes obvious. Such zig-zag mapping makes accurate analysis of religious participation possible for most of the nineteenth and all of the twentieth century – a task difficult or impossible to achieve so comprehensively elsewhere in the world.

A series of examples helps to demonstrate this. In each of these, census data are used combining morning and evening church attendances (excluding Sunday school attendances) across denominations on a particular Sunday, measured as a percentage of the population at large.[12] In some instances it is possible that there may be variations in the proportions of individuals attending both services (most church censuses count heads and not individuals). However, the overall levels of decline are too sharp to account for the decline solely in these terms. In addition, individual questionnaire data in the second half of the twentieth century confirm that fewer and fewer individuals go to church (and not simply that the same proportion of the population goes to church but less frequently).[13]

Churchgoing rates in London provide a clear indication of decline. In inner Greater London they amounted to 29.1 per cent in 1851, to 28.7 per cent in 1887, and then declined sharply to 22.4 per cent in 1903 and to just 10.7 per cent in 1989. Anglican attendances declined earliest there, from

---

[12] For sources and full data, see my *The Myth of the Empty Church* (London: SPCK, 1993).

[13] For data on this see my *Churchgoing and Christian Ethics* (Cambridge: Cambridge University Press, 1999).

15.6 per cent in 1851, to 14.1 per cent in 1887, to 9.6 per cent in 1903, and then to just 1.8 per cent in 1989. Free Church attendances, combined, increased from 11.3 per cent in 1851, to 12.5 per cent in 1887, but then declined to 10.7 per cent in 1903, and to 4.6 per cent in 1989. Roman Catholic attendances were just 2.3 per cent in 1851, had grown to 4.7 per cent in 1979, but then declined to 4.2 per cent in 1989. In Greater London the sharp recent decline of Roman Catholic atten-dances can be mapped more fully still: there they declined from 4.9 per cent in 1979, to 4.5 per cent in 1989, and to 3.3 per cent in 1998.[14]

In Liverpool, with a much larger Roman Catholic popu-lation, churchgoing rates have long been considerably higher than those in London. Nevertheless, there has been a similar pattern of churchgoing decline there – first amongst Anglicans, then amongst the Free Churches and finally amongst Roman Catholics. Overall churchgoing rates there were 39.9 per cent in 1851, 32.9 per cent in 1881, 31.9 per cent in 1891, 29.4 per cent in 1902, and 26.6 per cent in 1912. By 1989 overall atten-dances in Merseyside as a whole had declined to just 14 per cent. Anglican attendances declined sharply from 15.3 per cent in 1851, to 9.8 per cent in 1881, and then to 7.7 per cent in 1912. Free Church attendances increased to 12.7 per cent in 1881, then declined to 11.9 per cent in 1891, and to 8.7 per cent in 1912. With a large Irish workforce, Roman Catholic attendances in Liverpool already amounted to 13.9 per cent in 1851: in Merseyside as a whole they were still 11.5 per cent in 1979, but then they declined to 8.9 per cent in 1989. In an area incorporating Lancashire, Greater Manchester and Cheshire, as well as Merseyside, Roman Catholic attendances have continued to decline sharply from 8.1 per cent in 1979, to 6.7 per cent in 1989, and to 4.5 per cent in 1998.

York provides an instructive example of a smaller urban area with a more dominant Anglican Church. It is possible to map churchgoing patterns there accurately from 1837 until the present with remarkably few long gaps. At the start of this period,

---

[14] Data from the 1998 census (which are not contained in my earlier books) are calculated in this chapter from Peter Brierley (ed.), *UK Christian Handbook Religious Trends 2000/2001 No. 2* (London: Christian Research/HarperCollins, 1999).

Anglican attendances amounted to 16.8 per cent of the population. They had increased to a high 26.0 per cent in 1851, but then declined to 20.7 per cent in 1865, to 17.0 per cent in 1884, to 11.1 per cent in 1912, to 8.6 per cent in 1931, to 4.8 per cent in 1953, and to 3.4 per cent in 1989. Free Church attendances in York amounted to 19 per cent in 1837, but had declined to 13 per cent in 1901, to 5 per cent in 1935, and to 3 per cent in 1989. In 1837 these Free Church attendances were almost entirely Methodists, whereas in 1989 only half were. In proportion to the population of York, Methodist attendances, now just a twelfth of what they were a century-and-a-half earlier, have experienced the sharpest decline of any denomination. In contrast, Roman Catholic attendances in York amounted to 3.4 per cent in 1837, increased to 6.6 per cent in 1851, but then declined to 4.9 per cent in 1901, to 3.9 per cent in 1948, and remained at 4.1 per cent in 1989. Taken together, attendances at morning and evening church services across denominations in York, having risen from 39.2 per cent in 1837, declined from a high point of 50.6 per cent in 1851 to just 10.9 per cent in 1989. So, if London and Liverpool experienced almost a threefold decline in overall attendances between 1851 and 1989, in York the decline was nearer fivefold.

Another way of illustrating this long-term decline in religious participation is to compare statistics from a single denomination over a period of time. The official statistics published by the Church of England since the 1960s serve this purpose well (of course, if taken in isolation, without the statistics just reported for London, Liverpool and York, they seem to support Callum Brown's thesis that it was not until the 1960s that church decline started). Clergy-estimated 'average' or 'usual' Sunday attendances were recorded without interruption from 1968 until 1995. There was then a gap for two years (for reasons which will be discussed in a moment) before they were recorded again for 1998 and 1999. They point to continuous decline: they represented 3.5 per cent of the population in 1968, 3.0 per cent in 1973, 2.7 per cent in 1978, 2.5 per cent in 1985, 2.4 per cent in 1989, 2.1 per cent in 1995 and just 1.9 per cent in 1999. The sharpest decline has been among those aged under sixteen (declining by a third between 1986 and 1999). The proportion of infant baptisms in the Church of England to live births in the total population declined more sharply still: 67 per cent in 1950, 55 per cent in 1960, 47 per cent in 1970, 37 per cent in 1980, 28 per cent in 1990 and 21 per cent in 1999. Similarly, Easter Communions in the Church of England amounted to 8.4 per cent of the population aged over 15 in 1885 (rising to 9.8 per cent in 1911), but by 1999 they represented just 3 per cent of this population (and 3.1 per cent at Christmas). More dramatically, confirmations in the Church of England declined more than sixfold during the twentieth century. In 1911, 244,000 people were confirmed (representing 38 per cent of those aged 15), by 1960 this had declined somewhat to 190,000, but by 1980 it was 98,000 and by 1999 it was just 37,000.

Of course the Church of England is not alone. Until the 1960s, Roman Catholic statistics rose in contrast to other Churches in Britain. However, since then, Catholics nationally have shown a very sharp pattern of decline.[15] MARC Europe shows a national decline in Catholic attendances from 4.3 per cent of the total population in 1979 to just 2.5 per cent in 1998. It also shows that the average size of Catholic all-age attendances per church shrank in the period 1989–98 from 449 to 326. Michael Hornsby-Smith[16] also shows that mass attendances in England and Wales declined from 1,934,853 in 1970 to 1,461,074 in 1985. Hornsby-Smith produces the interesting statistic that, in the 1930s, 72 per cent of Catholics married other Catholics, whereas in the 1970s, only 31 per cent did. In other words, as they increasingly intermarry with the population at large in Britain, Catholics seem to be emulating the non-churchgoing habits of others. *Catholic Directory* average mass attendance statistics for England and Wales suggest an even sharper decline, from 4.1 per cent of the total population in 1964 to 2.1 per cent in 1998 (with only about a quarter of those identifying themselves as Catholics now attending mass regularly).[17] Similarly, communicant membership of the Church of Scotland has more than halved in proportion to the population of Scotland during the twentieth century.

Yet another way is to compare sample data from attitude surveys. It is now possible to make a number of crucial

[15] See *The Myth of the Empty Church*, ch. 8.

[16] Michael Hornsby-Smith, *Roman Catholicism in England* (Cambridge: Cambridge University Press, 1987).

[17] See Gordon Heald, 'Where Have All the Catholics Gone?', *The Tablet*, 19/6/1999, pp. 860–63.

comparisons from this data over the last fifty years.[18] In response to the question 'Would you describe yourself as being of any religion or denomination?' 23 per cent of a 1950 sample responded negatively. By 1983 this no-religion group (using data from *British Social Attitudes*) had grown to 31 per cent and by 1998 to 45 per cent. In the 1950s there was very little difference between age groups, yet by the 1990s there was a very striking difference: those aged 65 and over had changed little, but two-thirds of the 18–24 age group now gave a no-religion response. The Brierley *English Church Census* also suggests that support for the churches declined fastest amongst the young between 1979 and 1998. Whereas overall adult attendances in this period declined from 11.7 per cent of the adult population to 7.5 per cent, among children under fifteen the decline was more dramatic, from 14.5 per cent of the child population to 7.1 per cent (among those aged 65 and over it was only from 14.1 per cent to 11.7 per cent). The decline among Anglican children was sharper still – from 4.6 per cent to 1.8 per cent.

With this declared secularity there is now clear evidence of a general decline in Christian beliefs within the British population, as well as a marked increase in scepticism. Measuring these changes using data from more than one hundred national surveys conducted since the 1940s, it is now possible to map them with some accuracy. For example, a generalized belief in God shows some evidence of change, declining from a belief held by fourth-fifths of the population to two-thirds. However, stated disbelief increased sharply from just a tenth of the population to over one-quarter. The more specifically Christian belief in a personal God also shows clear signs of change, declining from a belief held in the 1940s by 43 per cent of the population to just 31 per cent in the 1990s. Belief in Jesus as the Son of God declined from just over two-thirds of the population to under one-half, whereas belief that Jesus was 'just a man' or 'just a story' increased from under one-fifth to some two-fifths of the population. A generalized belief in life after

---

[18] For this and subsequent unspecified attitude survey data see again my *Churchgoing and Christian Ethics*. An earlier version of some of these data was reported in Robin Gill, C. Kirk Hadaway and Penny Long Marler, 'Is Religious Belief Declining in Britain', *Journal for the Scientific Study of Religion* 37:3 (1998), pp. 507–16.

death is still held by something less than half of the population, but disbelief has doubled over the fifty years, now almost matching belief.

An Official Church of England Response

How have leaders in the Church of England responded to this evidence? The dominant reaction has been to attempt to deny it, most notably by questioning the statistics upon which it is based and, beyond that, by considerable confusion about what it means to 'belong' to an established Church. The recent official document *Statistics: a Tool for Mission* provides striking evidence of this response.

As mentioned earlier, 'usual' Sunday attendance statistics were not published for 1996 or 1997. A number of journalists at the time suspected that this was because church officials considered news of continuous recent decline to be damaging to morale in the Church. *Statistics: a Tool for Mission*, which reported after a wide-ranging review and consultation, gave different reasons for the decision: those under sixteen had not previously been included in the count; 'there is anecdotal evidence that week-on-week attendances are more variable now than in past years, and a simple average across all the weeks in the year, excluding festivals and holidays, may not adequately represent the overall attendance figures';[19] congregations at occasional offices are not included; variability within and between dioceses in methods of calculation; links with financial calculations can act as a disincentive to count attendances accurately. Most of these would be reasons for adjusting procedures rather than discontinuing the collection of these statistics. From the subsequent commentary it is clear that the reason quoted here in full was considered to be the most important. The following specific example is given from a diocesan survey:

> Research in the Diocese of Wakefield provided a snapshot of the broader picture of numbers of attenders and patterns

[19] *Statistics: a Tool for Mission* (London: Church House Publishing, 2000), p. 18.

of churchgoing. A register of every person who attended a church service was taken over an 8-week period from October to December 1997 in 17 parishes ... It was observed that 3,432 individuals attended a church service at some time during that period; this is 41 per cent higher than the usual Sunday attendance figure. In contrast, only 144 people (4 per cent) attended on all eight Sundays. (There were also 51 people who attended a midweek service, but not a Sunday service.) [20]

On the basis of this and two other similar local surveys, the report concludes that 'as a sole measure of church attendance, adult usual Sunday attendance no longer seems appropriate'. However, the problem with this conclusion is that it introduces the comparative phrase 'no longer' when it has cited only synchronic and not diachronic (or longitudinal) data. As mentioned earlier, there are several other measures that can be and have been used to compare diachronic practice within the Church of England – all of which unambiguously demonstrate institutional decline. On the basis of 'anecdotal' evidence alone it is suggested in the report that there has been a shift towards irregular churchgoing rather than a decline in churchgoing itself among those who still consider themselves to be church-goers. In contrast, both the Church of England's own statistics quoted earlier and opinion polls since the 1940s suggest that irregular churchgoing has long characterized a sizeable (but now declining) proportion of the population. [21] In any case, the level of decline from the mid-nineteenth century already mapped out in relation to London, Liverpool and York, and for Bromley during the twentieth century, shows quite clearly that churchgoing within the Church of England has declined in absolute terms.

It has long been a feature of democratic governments that, when they dislike public data pointing to *changing worlds*, they tend to alter the basis upon which the data are collected, arguing that they no longer represent the world as it is (totalitarian governments, of course, can either ignore or fabricate

---

[20] *Statistics: a Tool for Mission*, p. 19.
[21] See again my *The Myth of the Empty Church*.

data). By making such alterations they can then hope to avoid comparative judgements showing an increase in unemployment or whatever. Yet the danger is that this either (successfully) masks the problem both from themselves and from the public at large or (unsuccessfully) simply makes this public more cynical than ever about politicians. By proposing a new method for calculating 'average weekly attendance' (as it is now to become) the Church of England may be following a similar path.

The report also points to a wider confusion caused by the notion of an established Church. It reviews a number of legal and theological accounts of 'belonging' in the Church of England and concludes as follows:

> ... being baptized, being confirmed, joining the electoral roll, going to a Sunday service regularly every week, or taking communion at Christmas and Easter, are all part of a complex picture that describes the countable ways that people choose to belong. Parts of the picture, used in isolation, tell only part of the story. There are approximately 25 million people living in England who were baptized in Church of England churches. This tells us something about the Church, but so does the size of the electoral roll (currently 1.3 million) and so does the number of Easter communicants (approximately 1.2 million in 1997). Recognizing that there are different ways of belonging challenges the Church to define an appropriate strategy for mission and ministry.[22]

While the hierarchy of the Church of England still thinks in terms of establishment it is perhaps inevitable, as Casanova suggests, that such confusion will remain. Seen in terms of establishment, everyone in England is a parishioner of the Church of England and is represented in the House of Lords by its bishops. Seen in Catholic terms, rather, it is baptized Anglicans who constitute the Church of England, whether or not they subsequently attend any church services. Yet seen in the context of a pluralist, modern society – that is, in more denominational terms – it is those taking part regularly in worship who will be seen as the central focus. From this last

[22] *Statistics: a Tool for Mission*, p. 15.

perspective, looser forms of belonging will be welcomed when they are stages towards regular worship but distrusted when they become paths away from that worship. *Statistics: a Tool for Mission* avoids this last conclusion.

An alternative strategy might be instead to face data about institutional decline more directly and to seek to identify ways in which usual Sunday attendances might be increased in reality (including perhaps disestablishment). But to achieve that it is important to make distinctions, to identify some of the factors that may contribute to churchgoing decline and growth, and then to test them more rigorously. The next chapter will turn to these crucial tasks.

7

Beyond Decline – Three Case-studies

Long-term institutional decline is one of the most serious problems facing many Western churches. It is hardly surprising that so many church leaders have been tempted to ignore evidence of this decline and to clutch at straws instead. Perhaps statistics of decline are misleading or perhaps they are gathered on the wrong basis. Perhaps they have reached a plateau and will shortly be reversed. Perhaps people will come to their senses and a majority (or even a sizeable minority) will become regular churchgoers. Perhaps churches will become full again and the Victorian vision of an active church and priest for every community, however small, will be achieved. Perhaps cynicism will evaporate to be replaced by a new confidence in churches. The temptations here are obvious. A perennial reaction to *changing worlds* is to hope that by closing one's eyes all will be restored and that unwelcome changes will simply disappear.

A different way is to adopt as rigorous methods as possible in order to analyse the conditions in which churches might flourish, using the different skills and insights of sociologists, anthropologists, historians, management experts and church-growth specialists. This is not an easy task for several reasons. Obviously there is the practical task of keeping up to date in different literatures and then of acquiring sufficient competence to read them critically. However, there is also the problem of steering paths through the considerable differences of opinion within each of these areas. As ever, experts do not agree with each other, so critical judgements have to be made. Differences among sociologists of religion have already been noted in the previous chapter, but differences among anthropologists, management experts, historians and church-growth specialists can be just as sharp.

There are at least three levels at which such analysis can be made. At the macro-level, an attempt is made to understand the large-scale social processes that affect church growth and decline but over which churches themselves have little or no control. The quantitative skills of the sociologist and the social historian are particularly important here. At the micro-level, the concern is to identify the factors that induce individuals to change, either from being non-churchgoers to becoming churchgoers, or vice versa. Often the qualitative skills of the social anthropologist are more relevant here. At the intermediate level, an attempt is made to discover cultural factors promoting church decline or growth. These can be the very practical factors identified by management or church-growth specialists or they can be the more theoretical concepts of sociologists or social historians. An example of the latter has been noted earlier, namely Callum Brown's claim that the cultural changes of the 1960s had a radical effect upon institutional churches.[1] In late Victorian times it was more likely to be the invention of the bicycle or popular entertainment that were blamed for empty churches.[2]

Since I have written extensively about the possibilities of church growth at the intermediate level elsewhere,[3] the present chapter will focus upon the macro- and micro-levels. Through three international case-studies, my concern is to identify more clearly the context in which churches might still grow even in the modern world. Two of the case-studies will attempt to test how radical population changes can affect church growth, whereas the third will examine some of the idiosyncratic factors encouraging wholly secular young people to become regular churchgoers in modern China.

The first two case-studies build upon my research first started in *The Myth of the Empty Church*. There I argued that the massive population growth and urbanization of the first half of the nineteenth century presented churches with a major opportunity for growth. First the Free Churches and then the Anglican Church responded to these radical population changes with an energetic and largely successful building

---

[1] Callum G. Brown, *The Death of Christian Britain* (London: Routledge, 2001).

[2] See my *The Myth of the Empty Church* (London: SPCK, 1993).

[3] See my *Beyond Decline* (London: SCM Press, 1988) *A Vision for Growth* (London: SPCK, 1994), and (with Derek Burke) *Strategic Church Leadership* (London: SPCK, 1996).

campaign, comparable only to that of the Normans in the eleventh and twelfth centuries. However, the rapid suburban-ization and population shifts away from both the countryside and city centres that characterized the end of the nineteenth century presented many denominations with a major problem that endured throughout the twentieth century. In the countryside, churches and chapels (sometimes built or restored even in a context of rapid rural depopulation) increasingly struggled to have viable congregations or stipendiary ministers. In an urban context, first city-centre churches, next inner-city churches and then inner-suburban churches, lost their middle-class churchgoers as the latter moved further and further into suburbia.

Local-history studies have continued to illustrate this process. To take a London example, in *The Myth of the Empty Church* I showed extensively how the City of London churches were affected by population changes over a period of three hundred years. In 1700 an almost equal number of churches and chapels belonging to the Church of England and Independent Churches had a total seating capacity for 45 per cent of the population of the City of London. However, following rapid depopulation, Anglicans alone had seating capacity for 46 per cent of the population in 1801 and for 208 per cent in 1901. It is hardly surprising that in 1851 churches on average were only about a third full on a Sunday and that in the twentieth century there were five separate commissions attempting to find a role for largely redundant, but architecturally exquisite, churches. In turn, the historian Jeffrey Cox's pioneering study, *The English Churches in a Secular Society: Lambeth 1870–1930*,[4] showed how the large and once vigorous Anglican inner-city churches in Lambeth were affected by a late-nineteenth-century migration of the middle classes into the new suburbs. Next Jeremy Morris in his detailed study of the inner-suburban churches in Croydon[5] makes it possible to see another stage of this population shift, with churches there in the early twentieth century again losing many of their middle-class churchgoers

[4] Oxford: Oxford University Press, 1982.
[5] *Religion and Urban Change: Croydon 1840–1914* (Woodbridge, Suffolk: Boydell Press, 1992).

and consequently much of their vigour and position in local civic society. The situation of suburban Bromley considered in chapter 5 is surely part of the same process. Bromley remains an area of comparative affluence and higher-than-average churchgoing, but it too has finally succumbed to the church-going decline prevalent elsewhere – perhaps for no better reason now than that an ever-shifting population has gradually lost the habit of regular churchgoing.

Another important feature at the macro-level involves immigration. A sociological macro-level understanding of church growth and immigration can take a weaker or a stronger form. The weaker form argues that immigrants from high churchgoing countries typically retain these high rates for a while in their host country even if the latter has a low church-going rate. On this understanding, fresh immigrants find that church services (especially if they are in their mother tongue) are an important element helping them to retain a sense of identity in a foreign country. However, over time successive generations – losing their sense of strangeness and increasingly intermarrying with the host population – tend gradually to conform to the churchgoing level of the host country. Conversely, immigrants from low churchgoing countries will at first appear very different from the host population in a high churchgoing country, but will over time tend to adopt similar practices themselves.

A stronger version of these links is that ethnic churchgoing can become more important for immigrants facing problems of identity than it was in their original country, regardless of whether the host population has a high or low pattern of churchgoing itself.

Examples can readily be given of both the weak and strong version of this possible link between immigration and church-going. Irish Roman Catholic immigrants in England, during the nineteenth and first half of the twentieth century, clearly showed at least the weak version. English Roman Catholic churchgoing and church-building patterns (with just a single much-used church where other denominations would typically have three) were substantially shaped by these Irish immigrants.[6] As already

---

[6] See my *The Myth of the Empty Church.*

seen in the previous chapter, until intermarriage with the host population became dominant in the second half of the twentieth century, Roman Catholics in England largely resisted the relentless churchgoing decline experienced first by the Church of England from the middle of the nineteenth century and then by the Free Churches towards the end of the nineteenth century. Up until the 1960s, Roman Catholics, in an overall context of church decline, came to represent a more and more significant proportion of British churchgoers. Yet afterwards, as already noted, they have come to share the same fate as others. Now it is British Muslims who are the immigrant people to have a significantly higher level of religious participation than the British as a whole. Another recent example is Caribbean immigrants in Black Pentecostal churches. In the East End of London there does seem to be evidence that they now considerably raise the low level of local churchgoing.[7]

A rather stronger version of the possible link may be provided by patterns of churchgoing amongst the British in Hong Kong. A combination of the evangelical St Andrew's and the broad-church Cathedral does seem to attract a higher level of participation among British immigrants than might be expected back in Britain, albeit in a new context that is overwhelmingly non-Christian.

In the first case-study I will ask whether the stronger version of this macro-level process can be seen among British immigrants in Malta today. As immigrants, do they adopt the high levels of churchgoing of the Maltese themselves? In the second case-study I will turn to one of the prime examples of church growth in the late twentieth century, namely South Korea, to see whether or not it can be understood at a macro-level as relating to population growth and urbanization.

It will emerge that neither of these case-studies finally yields clear evidence of current church growth. However, the third case-study does. In mainland China, following the easing of restrictions upon mainline religions in 1981, many religious institutions have been experiencing a considerable resurgence. This particular case-study is primarily based upon interviews

---

[7] See Greg Smith, 'Religion, Ethnicity and Inter-faith Encounter', *Journal of Contemporary Religion* 13/3 (1998).

with teenage Catholics in Beijing, most of whom have joined the Church from almost wholly secular backgrounds. Naturally, they speak for themselves. Unlike macro-level quantitative studies that seek to map trends but cannot speak for all individuals (however dramatic the social trends there are always individuals who resist them), micro-level qualitative studies examine individual narratives in order to provide depth and nuance. Yet through such qualitative study, narratives may emerge from which others can learn and which may resonate with narratives from quite different contexts and cultures.

Case-study One – Malta

British immigrants in Malta provide an important case-study both because Malta has one of the highest indigenous regular churchgoing rates in the world (with four out of five Maltese claiming to go regularly to Mass) and because there has been a substantial and well-documented presence of British expatriates there for the last two hundred years.

During the first half of the nineteenth century it was noted at several points that a sizeable British population in Malta was ill-served by church buildings. Although there was an abundance of Roman Catholic churches (there are still some 330), there were very few non-Roman Catholic churches. As a result, in 1814 civil servants in London suggested that the central Roman Catholic church of St John in Valletta, elaborately built by the Knights of St John (which is today the Roman Catholic Co-Cathedral), should be taken over instead for Anglican worship. In response the British Governor in Malta wrote:

> At present time and I own my opinion clearly is that it would be inexpedient to insist upon this measure ... it appears that it would be a measure militating most severely against the prejudices of the people here, were we to insist of adopting as our own a place of worship which has been celebrated for ages as one of the first of the Roman Catholic persuasion.[8]

---

[8] See PRO Kew CO.158/40, and quoted in Alan Keighley, *Queen Adelaide's Church, Malta*, privately published by the author and sold by St Paul's Anglican Pro-Cathedral, Malta, 2000, p. 5.

Since the French had proved so unpopular with the Maltese in the 1790s because, amongst other indiscretions, they had expropriated treasures from their churches, it is hardly surprising that the British Governor was so alarmed. Tempting as it might have been to take over this magnificent, central building, it would have been deeply imprudent. He must have been aware that an island people who had so successfully ousted the French in 1800 could now make life extremely uncomfortable for their new British rulers once their religious sensibilities were upset.

The result was that when Queen Adelaide, the recent widow of William IV, came to Malta a quarter of a century later she was shocked to find that even then so little provision had been made for Anglican churchgoers. Two weeks after arriving for a winter of recuperation, she wrote about 'the want of a Protestant church in this place':

> There are so many English residents here, it is the seat of an English Government, and there is not one church belonging to the Church of England ... The consequence of this want of church accommodation has been that the Dissenters have established themselves in considerable number, and one cannot blame persons for attending their meeting when they have no church of their own.[9]

With a British civilian population of some 2,000, and 3,000 British troops in addition, there was strong pressure to build a substantial Anglican church. As in England at the time,[10] the impetus to build was both a fear of the increase of Dissenters and a desire to meet the needs of a growing urban population. The Methodist Church was the first non-Roman Catholic denomination to build a church in Malta in 1824. Queen Adelaide was clearly worried that Methodists might prove too attractive for the British expatriates. Indeed, by 1843 the Methodists expanded again, selling their original church in Valletta to the Free Church of Scotland and building a new church in Floriana, and by 1857 the Church of Scotland had

---

[9] Letter held in Wignacourt Museum, Rabat, Malta, and quoted in Keighley, *Queen Adelaide's Church*, p. 12.
[10] See my *The Myth of the Empty Church*.

built St Andrew's Scots Church in Valletta. It was already clear to Anglicans that they needed to act and, with money largely provided by Queen Adelaide on her departure from Malta in 1839, they were able to do so. Work was soon begun on what was to become the classically proportioned St Paul's Anglican Pro-Cathedral, Valletta.

At the opening of St Paul's in 1844, *The Malta Times* reported:

As this is the first edifice built in Malta for the worship of the Divine Being, according to the rites of the Anglican Church, its conspicuous situation in an open square in the most quiet part of the city of Valetta [*sic*], is a circumstance. Instead of going, as formerly, to an obscure chamber, on the ground floor of the palace of the ancient Grand Masters, which suggested to the native people but a poor idea of religious zeal and feelings of our countrymen, the English Christian will now be seen walking in the open light of day, into an elegant edifice, where he may worship his God and manifest his convictions of the truth of his belief in the way most conducive to the object of public worship. Indeed, it may be said that the public worship of the Church of England was never, with any good effects, celebrated in Malta until the 1st of November, 1844, from which day we hope we may date the example and rapid progress of the true faith in that island.[11]

From this report it would seem that St Paul's was not simply to be a church for British expatriates. It was also to be seen as a chance to demonstrate 'the true faith' to the Roman Catholic Maltese.

In reality, though, the congregation at St Paul's has always consisted primarily of expatriates (both civilian and military) rather than Maltese and its fortunes have depended largely upon the changing fortunes of these expatriates. So, by 1931 the congregation was described as a 'small regular congregation of civilians'.[12] During the Second World War even this civilian expatriate population largely left Malta, returning to boost congregations only in 1946. However, by 1957 it was

---

[11] *The Malta Times*, 31 Dec. 1844, p. 115.
[12] *Minutes* (December 10th), held in the archives at St Paul's Anglican Pro-Cathedral, Valletta, Malta.

reported that 'congregations vary and as the large majority of those who attend the Cathedral are service personnel there is a context of change'.[13] Political independence, a decade later, was soon followed by the withdrawal of the British navy and, with it, a radical change of status both for St Paul's and for the smaller Holy Trinity, formerly the bishop's chapel, across the bay in Sliema. Alan Keighley notes that, 'faced with a decline in church attendances and financial problems, it was decided in 1983 that for administrative purposes the two churches should be combined [with] a single electoral roll'.[14]

The Free Churches faced similar problems caused by a fluctuating expatriate population. In 1974 the Methodists closed their church in Floriana, returning to Valletta to merge with St Andrew's Scots Church. Since 1991, the latter has also shared some of its facilities with a small German-speaking congregation of the EKD (the Evangelical Church of Germany). The minister at St Andrew's reported that over the twenty-five years of his ministry there, the congregation has lost three important constituents: British service people; young British people with work contracts; and the British immigrants of the late 1960s who, to comply with legislation then, spent most of their time at Malta. Today, in contrast, most British home-owners in Malta are retired and, with cheap air travel, spend only part of the year there.

Malta is also now a major tourist island with over a million tourists coming there every year. St Paul's, especially, sees many tourists during the week and quite a number on a Sunday too. Inter-church travel on occasions brings whole parties to services there, boosting the regular congregation. Increasing travel has also resulted in the growth of small, independent Evangelical, Adventist and Pentecostal congregations over the last two decades. Some of these have been started by Maltese, typically converted while living in the United States or Australia, who have then returned to Malta. There is evidence of considerable tension between them and their Catholic relatives. Others have been started by expatriate missionaries (often again from the United States) sponsored by their home denominations. My

---

[13] Ibid.
[14] Keighley, *Queen Adelaide's Church*, p. 163.

contact with five of these eleven congregations suggests that, perhaps not surprisingly, few of the retired and largely middle-class British expatriates join them. The few who do, typically have prior commitments to them before coming to Malta.

Naturally, some of the British expatriate are themselves Roman Catholic. Compared with British expatriates retirees in Tuscany, the Costa del Sol and the Algarve, those in Malta tend to be more elderly (on average 68 years old in one sample)[15] and less inclined than the others to learn the local language. In Malta, the British colonial connection, the island's strategic role in the Second World War, and Maltese labour migration to the United Kingdom, have all encouraged intermarriage. Never-theless, even British Roman Catholics marrying Maltese practising Roman Catholics tend not to learn much Maltese, relying rather upon the Maltese speaking to them instead in English. British Roman Catholic couples, retiring to Malta for the weather (a factor that many mentioned in a recent survey),[16] have even less reason for learning Maltese. As a result, the Roman Catholic Church in Malta has appointed an English-speaking chaplain who ministers specifically to them. So, like other British expatriates, they can live much of their social and religious life in an English-speaking enclave.

Language may not be the only problem for British Roman Catholic expatriates. The very culture of Maltese Catholicism may be strange to them, with its combination of traditional faith and very local piety. In his important study, *Saints and Fireworks: Religion and Politics in Rural Malta*, the anthropologist Jeremy Boissevain examines at length the role of the colourful *festas* that many churches celebrate, with their deep roots in local politics and community. These *festas* characteristically involve parading the statue of a church's saint around the parish after a special Mass, accompanied by a loud band, much feasting and fireworks. In his original 1965 study, Boissevain saw increasing signs of conflict between churches and society at large. However, by 1993 he had come to revise his views

---

[15] See Anthony M. Warnes, Russell King, Allan M. Williams and Guy Patterson, 'The Well-being of British Expatriate Retirees in Southern Europe', *Ageing and Society* 19 (1999), pp. 717–40.
[16] Ibid.

somewhat and was surprised to find that local church celebrations had actually increased in social significance:

> To my mind, the increase in certain celebrations – the *festas* of parish and neighbourhood patron saints and Passion Week – is a manifestation of a desire to celebrate the community. People, who have grown up together in poverty and are now separated by prosperity, wish to recreate, for a few moments, the feeling of solidarity, of togetherness, by celebrating – watching fireworks, dancing in the street, drinking, praying, visiting, walking behind the band, listening to music in the square.[17]

Of course British Roman Catholics in Malta may, like British tourists, view these *festas* with fascination. Some of those interviewed also expressed strong sympathy for the sense of family that they engendered. However, despite their common allegiance to Rome, they may still feel themselves to be relative strangers. A more familiar Mass said in English by an understanding chaplain may finally seem preferable.

Given this background, what evidence is there of the relative strength of churchgoing patterns amongst British expatriates in Malta today? And how do these patterns compare with the extraordinary level of Maltese churchgoing?

An initial problem is caused by the difficulty of accurately estimating the size of this British expatriate population. The increasing mobility of British expatriates makes it difficult to define accurately who is and who is not an immigrant. One person may spend all but two months in Malta, whereas another may be absent for ten months. Some might also be reluctant, for tax reasons, to be too specific about the proportion of the year that they do actually live in Malta. Nevertherless, local (highly approximate) estimates suggest that of the current population of Malta, of some 380,000 about 5,000 are British. If this estimate is at all accurate, it suggests that the overall British population in Malta is about the same as it was a century and a half ago (combining civilian and military populations then) whereas the overall Maltese population has more than trebled.

---

[17] Valletta, Malta: Progress Press, 1993, p. 158, (originally published by Athlone Press, University of London, 1965).

So, using these estimates, today British expatriates represent just 1.3 per cent of the total population of Malta, whereas once they represented 4.3 per cent.

Responses from local clergy[18] in May 2000 suggest that in a typical week some 7 per cent of the British expatriates attend an English-language Roman Catholic Mass, 4 per cent attend one of the four Anglican centres (the Pro-Cathedral at Valletta, the church at Sliema and small centres at Gozo and Mellieha) and 2 per cent the combined Presbyterian/Methodist St Andrew's Church in Valletta. The overall 13 per cent does not include British Roman Catholics who attend local Maltese churches, yet it does give some means of comparing expatriate and indigenous churchgoing rates in Malta. Even if approximate it clearly indicates that expatriate levels of churchgoing are very considerably lower than those of the Maltese themselves. A figure of 13 per cent is still higher than the 7.5 per cent of the 1998 English census,[19] but, since this is an elderly, middle-class population, it may not be especially high.

At most, then, the weaker version of the possible link between immigration and churchgoing seems to be at work here. A majority of British expatriates in Malta do not appear to emulate strongly the church involvement of the Maltese. Even if the 13 per cent churchgoing rate amongst British expatriates can be raised somewhat by tracing more elusive churchgoers, it still appears to be nowhere near the Maltese rate (even if only half of the four-out-of-five Maltese who claim to be regular Mass-goers are actually in church on a given Sunday).

The one exception may be British Roman Catholic expatriates. Roman Catholics do represent a proportionately larger group of churchgoers amongst British expatriates than they would typically in Britain (normally about a third of all churchgoers but here over a half). If Roman Catholic affiliation amongst British expatriates is similar to that in Britain (about 11 per cent), then the percentage of regular church-goers amongst them (77 per cent) would be very similar to that

[18] I am particularly grateful, amongst others, to Fr Charles Carabott, Rev. Colin Westmarland and Canon Alan Woods for their valuable help, and to the latter and his wife Barbara for their generous hospitality.
[19] See Peter Brierley (ed.), *UK Christian Handbook Religious Trends 2000/2001 No. 2* (London: Christian Research/HarperCollins, 1999).

of the Maltese. On this basis, there is a possibility that this particular group has been encouraged, through living in Malta, to become more active in churchgoing. Yet even here it is also possible that a disproportionate number of churchgoing Roman Catholic expatriates has been attracted to Malta in the first place by its high regard for traditional Catholicism. Malta is, after all, a country that was specifically commended for its faith by Pope John Paul II on his visit there in 1990.

Another variable in this difficult comparison concerns the Maltese themselves. There are currently reports in local newspapers of disaffection amongst younger Roman Catholics. For example, in a feature on problems facing young people, *The Malta Independent on Sunday* recently suggested:

> Giving a meaning to life is also believed to be found through the Church at times. Since Malta is strongly Catholic, the Church is in a position to help. Confusion and disillusionment of the Church are what discourage and make young people suffer. Youth centres are being frequented less here in Malta, mass on Sundays has a low percentage of young people attending – there must be a reason. Why are young people dissociating themselves from the Church?[20]

Whether this is an expression of the perennial belief that the young are uniquely becoming disaffected, or whether it is an indication that globalization is beginning to change traditional Maltese culture, remains to be seen. If it is the latter, then it is possible that the link between immigration and churchgoing may sometimes be the reverse of the patterns outlined earlier. The presence of pluralistic, largely non-churchgoing tourists and expatriates may provide a powerful counter-influence to family traditions for young Maltese. Since tourism now plays such a dominant part in the economy and employment in Malta, it may not be surprising if the young start to emulate the wider European culture they encounter in the process. And, since this wider European culture no longer includes church-going as a significant factor, the apparent disaffection of Maltese youth from their local churches may be a result.

---

[20] *The Malta Independent on Sunday*, 14 May 2000, p. 13.

It is wise not to jump to this conclusion too swiftly. Jeremy Boissevain's study acts as a clear warning about underestimating the resilience of Maltese Catholicism. It is not simply that he underestimated the significance of *festas*; he later also came to recognize that his original 1965 study had also overestimated the significance of the anti-clericalism fostered in the 1960s by political leaders such as Dom Mintoff. Some sections of Maltese society today are even keen to encourage the Roman Catholic Church to play a greater socio-political role. To return to *The Malta Independent on Sunday*, in a recent editorial it argued:

> The problem with the Catholic Church in Malta is that in the past it went from one extreme to another. In the 1960s it wrongly entered into battle against the Malta Labour Party and was excessively harsh in its criticism of the party. However, when in the 1970s and 1980s democracy was trampled on and human rights were eroded by the Labour government, the Church on the whole remained silent, possibly because it wanted to avoid a repetition of the politico-religious dispute of the 1960s. This was a wrong decision and showed poor leadership by the Church. Today the Church is speaking out somewhat on issues but can do much more. The Malta Labour Party should not criticise the Church for airing its views just because the position of the Church is somewhat different from its own. As an important institution in our country, the Catholic Church has every right to have its voice heard, regardless of whether the message is well-received by the politicians.[21]

I suspect that it is still too early to predict whether the religious culture of this island country will conform to the religious decline that is dominant elsewhere in Europe, or whether it will prove to be more resilient. If the former, then it will in effect gradually conform to the lower churchgoing rates of most of its immigrants and tourists. But if the latter, then perhaps the Roman Catholic immigrants may themselves tend to conform to the higher churchgoing rates of the Maltese.

Whichever scenario unfolds, however, it seems unlikely that non-Roman Catholic immigrants will be much affected. After two centuries, British non-Roman Catholic expatriates have

[21] *The Malta Independent on Sunday*, 14 May 2000, p. 18.

proved to be remarkably resistant to the religion, culture and language of the Maltese.

Case-study Two – South Korea

For at least thirty years South Korea has often been cited as a (perhaps even *the*) prime example of 'explosive' church growth. Members of evangelical congregations in the West have made frequent visits to Seoul to witness this phenomenon. In turn, Korean missionaries have been encouraged to come to the West to put new missionary energy into declining churches here. More broadly still, it is often claimed that there is unprecedented church growth in South Asia and Africa far outweighing the decline so apparent in Britain, Canada, Australia, New Zealand and most of Europe. Within this context, South Korea remains a shining counter-example to the claim that churches and modernity do not mix. South Korean churches, it seems, have managed to cope with *changing worlds* quite remarkably – combining a rapid transition into modern urbanization and the globalized economy with fast-expanding congregations. They have become the embodiment of the belief that church decline is not inevitable in the modern or postmodern world.

Measured in terms of their reported membership figures, South Korea did indeed see remarkable church growth following its liberation from Japan and the end of the Korean War. In 1970 Christians of all denominations represented less than one in ten of the South Korean population.[22] Two decades

[22] Statistics on church membership in South Korea can be found (in English) in Kwang-Soon Lee, 'Growth and Undergrowth of the Korean Church', *Korea Presbyterian Journal of Theology*, 1, 1 (May 2001), pp. 263–90 (published by Presbyterian College and Theological Seminary Press, Seoul); Sung-Ho Kim, 'Rapid Modernisation and the Future of Korean Christianity', *Religion* (forthcoming); and Byoung Suh Kim, 'Socio-Religious Analysis of the Korean Church: Modernization and Explosive Growth and Decline of Protestantism in Korea', paper given at the International Academy of Practical Theology Conference, Seoul, 22–26 April 1997. Church membership figures for the 1960s and 1970s are taken by them from *The Yearbook of Korean Religion* and for the 1980s and 1990s from the Korean National Statistics Office. However, it should be noted that, although they do not affect the broad points being made in this case-study, there are some discrepancies between the statistics reported by Kwang-Soon Lee, Sung-Ho Kim and Byoung Suh Kim.

later, this ratio had changed to one in four. The population of South Korea almost doubled between 1962 and 1994, but the reported membership of the Protestant Churches increased five times faster in that period from some 736,000 to a remarkable 8,146,000. The main Presbyterian Church of Korea (despite internal divisions) grew in two decades from representing just 2 per cent of the total population to almost 5 per cent, and, in the process, doubled its number of churches. The pattern of growth and size was very similar in the Roman Catholic Church. It is hardly surprising, then, that Christians from other countries came to see this phenomenal church growth at first hand, hoping no doubt to learn how it might be copied elsewhere.

However, Korean scholars such as Byoung Suh Kim, Kwang-Soon Lee and Sung-Ho Kim have begun to present a more complex picture than these bald statistics would seem to demonstrate. Many of those who have used South Korea as an example of 'explosive' church growth have failed to note a parallel and rather faster pattern of growth reported by Buddhists there. For example, their reported membership grew from just 687,000 in 1962 to 11,729,000 in 1991. Of course it is dangerous to compare this pattern of growth straightforwardly with that reported by Protestants. Membership figures are typically compiled either directly from the reported statistics of local congregations (who may have their own reasons for exaggerating) or from census data completed by householders (who may make assumptions about other members of their household). There is plenty of opportunity, especially in a rapidly changing country, for there to be considerable overlap between the membership lists of various Protestant and Buddhist denominations. It is even possible for individuals in South Asia to flirt simultaneously with both Protestantism and Buddhism in one form or another. Nor is it clear that different denominations within either Protestantism or Buddhism have similar criteria for establishing 'membership' (Anglicans worldwide notoriously do not). Elsewhere I have argued[23] that recorded attendances make much better comparators, at least within Christianity, than 'membership' figures (but sadly in

[23] See my *The Myth of the Empty Church*, ch. 1.

South Korea there is yet to be a national or even urban census of attendances). While clearly recognizing such difficulties, these Korean scholars argue nonetheless that apparent evidence of Buddhist resurgence should not simply be ignored.

Again, all three Korean scholars agree that, although rapid membership growth characterized Christians and Buddhists alike in South Korea from about 1960 to 1985, there has been membership stagnation or even decline during the 1990s. Sung-Ho Kim traces an actual decline among Buddhists, virtual stagnation among Protestants and only a very modest growth among Roman Catholics (whose rapid increase started rather later, in the 1970s, than Protestants or Buddhists). Kwang-Soon Lee describes the plight of Protestant Churches entering the new millennium as follows:

> After 100 years of the Korean Church mission, the remarkable trend of growth has slowed down. The great evangelical rallies and other smaller movements of the 1970s, which brought forth brisk developments, and snowballed into a reproductive course of rapid growth, by the beginning of the 1990s showed signs of deceleration. Finally at the close of the 20th century, the Korean Church reached the state where the nominal number of church members started to decrease. Such a phenomenon is unsettling a large number of people within the Korean Church. When reflecting on the Western Church of the latter half of the 20th century, especially the aging and collapse of the European Church, and the emptying out of the larger American urban churches, we can't help but to wonder if the symptoms we are now seeing are an indication that the Korean Church is in danger of following in the same footsteps.[24]

Within these academic circles at least there is a growing recognition that Korean churches are now facing a new situation of what is rather quaintly called 'aftergrowth' or even 'undergrowth'. Four years ago, Byoung Suh Kim was unusual in arguing that church growth had reached a plateau in the 1980s. Today there is wider recognition that the 1990s did not see the rapid growth in reported church membership of earlier

---

[24] Kwang-Soon Lee, 'Growth and Undergrowth', p. 263.

decades. Instead congregations now appear increasingly elderly and churches themselves have lost some of their popularity in the country as a whole (especially among the young).

Having acknowledged this new situation in the Korean churches in the 1990s, Kwang-Soon Lee makes a clear link between church growth and macro-level sociological factors. Some of these factors are very specific to South Korea. For example, she notes the new enthusiasm for all things Western, including Christianity, that emerged after liberation from Japan, an enthusiasm that is still present in a now elderly generation. Other factors, however, such as those connected to urbanization and suburbanization, closely match those of nineteenth-century Britain. So, she shows that in her own denomination, the Presbyterian Church of Korea, congregational growth has characterized urban rather than rural congregations, as rural areas have depopulated and urban areas expanded. Whereas in the Seoul Presbytery the size of an average congregation grew from 241 members in 1965 to 1,155 in 1995, in an Eastern rural Presbytery they actually declined from 378 to 249. Again, she notes that recent church growth has mainly been in suburban churches as populations (and churchgoers) move out from the centre of Seoul to the new satellite cities that surround it.

In summary, she argues:

> The growth of the Korean Church cannot be explained by any one variable, but it can be said that the unique circumstances of Korea, such as colonization, independence, war, anti-communism, along with the underlying interest towards Christianity, the fluctuation of social change brought by trends of urbanization and industrialization and the Korean Church's strong devotion and efforts in missions, all together collectively caused the effect of rapid growth.[25]

Kwang-Soon Lee studied for her doctorate at Fuller Theological Seminary so she is certainly not predisposed to favour sociological rather than theological explanations of church growth. Indeed, she discusses the latter in some detail. However, in words that may find an echo among assiduous

---

[25] Kwang-Soon Lee, 'Growth and Undergrowth', p. 282.

ministers and priests in areas of low churchgoing in Britain, she reaches an obvious conclusion:

> It is unsatisfactory to award all the merits to the great passion of evangelism as the causes for growth in the Korean Church. If the dedication to missions and effort were the causes for church growth, then this would mean that the other societies that did not show such growth were lacking that sort of zeal for missions, but is that really the case? Although there is a degree of difference ... the fact is that even in these non Christian areas, in almost all of them there are many people working in ministries who have a burning passion and are concentrating whole heartedly on mission efforts, but regardless, they do not show the same growth as the Korean Church.[26]

So, it does seem after all that, despite some very distinctive features, South Korean patterns of church growth and decline have affinities with those to be found elsewhere. More than that, churches there do not seem to be immune to the macro-level factors that shaped many Western churches. In her conclusion, Kwang-Soon Lee hopes that this is not the case and that Korean churches will still be able to grow. Yet the force of her argument is that growth will now be distinctly more difficult than it was in the 1960–85 period.

In another recent contribution, the theologian Sou-Yong Lee argues more bluntly that the Korean Church is now confronted with:

1. The situation of the division of North and South Korea, awaiting future reunification.
2. The situation in which the Korean church is asked to take on the leading role in world mission.
3. The situation in which the Korean church has to regain respect and love from the general Korean society.[27]

Doubtless, if eventual reunification of Korea is anything like that of Germany, then it will be extremely costly. Indeed, given the deep level of poverty in the North and the less-than-stable

---

[26] Kwang-Soon Lee, 'Growth and Undergrowth', p. 280.
[27] In a response at the Centenary Conference of the Presbyterian College and Theological Seminary, Seoul, May 2001.

economy in the South, there may well be very serious problems lying ahead for Korean churchgoers and non-churchgoers alike.

However, it is the second and third points that are especially important in terms of the present case-study. The high expectations of Western Churches encouraged South Korea to send and finance missionaries around the world (just as the British Churches did in the nineteenth century). Yet much of this activity is premised on an expanding Church that can afford to do this and is confident that it has the recipe for church growth. Not only is this confidence beginning to erode but there is also a fear that the Church in Korea no longer has the respect of society at large. A series of scandals involving the leaders of fundamentalist Christian groups has not helped. Their extravagant promises of spiritual, physical and economic wellbeing for their followers have proved less convincing following South Korea's economic crisis. A hardworking people may now be more suspicious of claims about 'growth' of any kind. The global world is a good deal tougher than many had expected. Indeed, by linking the work of the Holy Spirit so closely to church growth perhaps a serious distortion had been made in the past. Some conservative Korean Christians argue that the Holy Spirit has simply moved to China. Others rather see the Holy Spirit working in new and challenging ways in Korea, calling Christians to be more active in society at large. A leading Anglican priest has even become a member of the Korean Congress. And at the impressive Presbyterian College and Theological Seminary in Seoul, several theologians are now engaged in exploring new ways of doing theology that avoid fundamentalism and are relevant to the new Korea.

Case-study Three – China

Visits to churches in Beijing and Xian in May 2001 soon confirmed two points. The first is that there is a massive programme of urban development taking place in modern China. The centre of Beijing is covered in dust from multiple building works as traditional hutongs are rapidly replaced with blocks of flats and apartments. Posters are displayed everywhere expressing the determination of Beijing to win the bid for the

2008 Olympic Games. City-centre industrial chimneys, which contributed to the urban pollution that destroyed (along with doubts about political freedom) the previous bid, are now smokeless. This is a city determined to modernize as fast as possible. The second point is that many religious institutions are experiencing a very considerable period of rejuvenation. Since 1981, eighteen of the thirty Catholic churches closed during the Cultural Revolution have been reopened in Beijing, restored with State money, and are reporting well-attended services. At the Catholic Southern Cathedral there are now four masses every Sunday (one in Latin, two in Chinese and one in English) with capacity or near-capacity congregations. At the even-larger Catholic Northern Cathedral there are several masses on a Sunday, each with some two thousand people present, a third of them young people. Protestants are also actively restoring former churches, but, in addition, they are currently opening new ones as well. One packed Protestant congregation visited in Beijing had, in addition to its usual services, a Sunday afternoon service for Koreans living there. In a new church visited in Xian, seats were tightly packed together in order to make enough room for a growing congregation. An older, restored Protestant church visited there has to relay its services to a hall next door in order to accommodate all those who wish to attend its services. A Buddhist temple in Xian reported a very similar experience, with thousands attending festivals, and the Great Mosque in Xian is visibly and actively used for daily prayer and Friday worship by the sizeable local Muslim community there.

It is too early to get reliable religious statistics in modern China. The religious rejuvenation there is still too recent and some nervousness about religious freedom remains. While mainstream denominations across different religious traditions are no longer persecuted as they were during the Cultural Revolution, there is still considerable defensiveness about movements such as Falun Gong. For example, the English-language newspaper *China Daily* is anxious to stress that religious freedom is enjoyed by all people in China and is sharply critical of the 2001 annual report of the US Commission on International Religious Freedom, which claimed otherwise. It extensively reports the views of religious leaders who support this position rather than the views of those who dissent from it. The following is just one example:

Fu Tiesham, chairman of the Chinese Patriotic Catholic Association ... said the China-related part of the report 'distorted facts with ulterior motives' and was completely unacceptable. Catholic followers in China enjoy freedom of religion, he said. He described the US report as a sheer fabrication and an attempt to call white black, which violates the basic norms of international relations and grossly interferes in China's internal affairs. 'There is no way that religious figures like us would accept it,' he said. As for Falun Gong, Fu said it is not a religion at all but an evil cult that is against human beings, science and society. He went on to say that by attempting to speak for such a cult, the US aims to destabilize China and hinder its economic development.[28]

After discussions with a number of religious leaders, there can be little doubt that they do still feel a need to tread carefully in modern China. Catholic, Protestant and Buddhist leaders all reported similar experiences during the Cultural Revolution. Those brought up in religiously observant families were told by their parents to tell nobody outside their family about their religious faith. Middle-aged Catholics and Protestants alike could still remember as children praying and reading the Bible secretly in fear of local, political authorities. A Buddhist abbot reported that he had to memorize by heart the Scriptures owned for generations by his family before they were burned. A Catholic priest vividly recalled the emotional experience of his family attending their first public Mass in years at the reopening of the Northern Cathedral.

Given these experiences, it would be unrealistic to expect the kind of religious statistics to be found in South Korea. Mainline religious institutions in China are still cautious in their dealings with the State and the State, in turn, continues to seek a degree of control over these religious institutions. Nevertheless, within the controlled parameters of those denominations currently 'allowed' by the State there is plentiful anecdotal evidence both of current rejuvenation and a sense of newfound freedom. It is certainly possible today to talk openly with members and leaders of such denominations in public places.

[28] *China Daily*, Beijing, 7 May 2001, p. 4

The current pattern of religious rejuvenation and liberation does have parallels with that experienced in South Korea during the 1960–85 period. The cultural transition and rapid urbanization/modernization accompanied by the growth of religious institutions appears to fit a similar pattern. The macro-level factors identified in the previous case-study do indeed seem to be relevant. The sort of rapid urbanization and accompanying religious energy evident in nineteenth-century Britain and twentieth-century South Korea does seem to characterize twenty-first-century China. Yet there are also at least two macro-level differences. The one-child policy of urban China has attempted to avoid the sort of rapid population growth that characterized Britain and South Korea during their periods of rapid urbanization and rural depopulation. And the liberation following the Cultural Revolution in China, unlike the South Korean liberation from Japanese rule, was an internal liberation from an aggressively secular culture.

It is in this macro-level context that the qualitative interviews with seven teenagers, four girls and three boys, from the Catholic Southern Cathedral took place. A central concern of the interviews was to establish in their own words the factors that had persuaded them to become churchgoers. Together, they formed a group of friends within the Cathedral, all were without siblings, all were clearly intelligent, articulate and actively learning English at school (most could respond well in English themselves and translate for the few who were more diffident), all had grown up in Beijing and only one came from a Catholic family. Overwhelmingly, this was a group of urban young people from a very secular background who for one reason or another had become churchgoing Catholics. They looked like teenagers anywhere in the world, dressed in colourful tee-shirts, trainers, hair-bands and jeans. There was not a Maoist suit in sight: this is definitely a post-Cultural Revolution generation. The relaxed atmosphere of a shared meal in a public restaurant allowed them to talk quite freely about their distinctive experiences. Naturally, like teenagers everywhere, they teased each other and laughed and joked, but they were also keen to tell an outsider in detail why they had made this transition from the secular to the religious.

All of the six teenagers who had become Catholics from secular backgrounds reported that this had been a gradual process, in one case taking six years. Perhaps because they were Catholics and not evangelical Protestants they were encouraged by their priests to think in terms of a process of catechism rather than a single-point declaration of Christian conversion. During the English Mass at the Southern Cathedral the presiding priest specifically invited 'believers' to receive the sacrament and 'non-believers' to show respect by not doing so. In conversations afterwards it became clear that a proportion of any congregation is likely to consist of those who are observing the service with a possible view to joining one of the large catechism classes later. In a political context in which public proselytism is still forbidden, 'observers' within congregations become an important source of new members.

But what attracted these young people to become such 'observers' in the first place? Here their experiences were quite varied. One of the boys talked at length about his search for meaning and purpose in life. He felt that there must be more to life than material things. All of the others agreed with this and none laughed when he made this statement. These were serious and thoughtful young people. Perhaps the fact that they were only-children made them more introspective than they might have been in households with siblings. Yet none of this explains why they chose to find meaning and purpose specifically within the Catholic Church.

To account for this, all of them offered more mundane, but often multi-layered, explanations. Friendships were clearly important. One girl explained that she joined the catechism class together with her mother after extensive conversations with a friendly Catholic neighbour. Another girl said that friendship with one of the other girls in this group had been an important factor. However, even here it was not the only and certainly not the initial factor. She said that she first started to become interested in Christianity through listening to hymns broadcast on the radio from evangelical churches in Hong Kong. After several years of doing this secretly on her own, she decided to investigate churches more directly as the new millennium approached. Given that it was evangelical worship she had found attractive on the radio, it might have been logical for her to join a Protestant church in Beijing. But it was her girl friend, already a member of the congregation at the

Southern Cathedral, who drew her to that specific church. In all, this process had taken some six years. That in itself may indicate something of the difficulty that an individual faces when crossing the various thresholds involved here, especially in a radically secularized culture. It is one thing to enjoy hymns on the radio, but it is another to make a cognitive connection with Christian faith, and it is another again to become a churchgoer with a group of strangers.

The attraction of church music was mentioned by several of the young people. But how had they come to hear this music in the first place? Listening to the radio from Hong Kong was only one experience. More typical were reports of first hearing this music at the Midnight Mass at Christmas. The route to this was quite unexpected. All reported that it is popular today for young people to exchange Christmas cards and even presents in Beijing. As a result, some young people become curious about the origins of this custom and start to make links to churches. In a Protestant church visited in Xian these links are made quite flamboyantly, with two huge display posters stored in the annexe to the church waiting for another Christmas. One of these portrays a conventional Victorian picture of a blond, long-haired, blue-eyed Jesus as a shepherd (in stark contrast to the Chinese Madonna in the Northern Cathedral in Beijing). The other is simply Santa Claus together with reindeer, sledge and snow. The juxtaposition curiously reverses the usual complaint by Western Christians that Christmas is becoming too secular and commercial. Ironically, in modern China a secularized, commercialized Christmas has become a carrier of Christian memories that can then be exploited by churches. As a result, services at Christmas time have become surprisingly popular well beyond the boundaries of church membership.

Another obvious source for Christian memories is literature. Several of the young people mentioned that they had first made links with Christianity through their reading. One girl, for example, said that she became curious initially after reading about Noah's Ark in a novel. One of the boys talked about an early attempt to read the New Testament. Again, as intelligent only-children, it may not be too surprising that the introspective world of private reading is a significant factor here. Biblical allusions that are simply taken for granted in a Western society, where Christian memories are fresher, may well appear more interesting and exotic in a China now liberated from the Cultural Revolution. In the Buddhist Temple visited in Xian, the number of young people immersed in the study of Buddhist Scriptures was again striking.

Nevertheless, young people who are churchgoers (and perhaps those who are religiously active in any form) are still very much a minority in Beijing. An outwardly secular life still appears to be the norm there. So do these young Catholics experience hostility either from their families or from their peers? This question was asked several times, but the young people were all emphatic that they did not experience hostility. As already mentioned, one girl came from a Catholic family and another had become a Catholic at the same time as her mother. However, none of the remaining five reported any hostility. Instead, their dominant experience from family or friends was simply a statement that it was 'up to them', it was their 'personal choice'. Perhaps for their parents or peers, religion was simply a privatized issue without any broader social significance. However, one girl said that after her own baptism she did try to persuade her parents to come with her to the Southern Cathedral. They were unwilling to do that, but they did subsequently ask her to pray for particular issues for them when she went to Mass. She concluded laconically that her parents were 'neither believers nor non-believers'.

Of course such qualitative data should not be used to make generalizations about China as a whole. The young people interviewed may or may not have been representative of other young people in Beijing, let alone of people in the rest of China. That is not the point of such micro-level data. Instead, qualitative data offer a fascinating glimpse of these particular young people as they experience the remarkable changes that are taking place in modern China. More than that, they offer suggestions about how it is still possible for young people within a radically secularized culture to make connections with conventional Christianity. The connections here are multi-layered and sometimes unexpected, involving a mixture of mundane and teleological factors. They are not irrelevant to the broad macro-level factors examined in the other two case-studies (these young people are indeed part of a rapidly urbanizing society), but they are still distinct from them. It is worth remembering that, however strong macro-level trends are, some individuals act against the flow of their peers. There are always some people who make religious connections even within the most radically secularized culture.

PART THREE

Changing Approaches to Theology

8

Beyond Confessional Theology

The first part of *Changing Worlds* looked at changing moral perceptions within churches, whereas the second examined changing patterns of churchgoing. However, *Changing Worlds* would be incomplete without also addressing changing ways of studying theology. For those engaged in the study of theology within the critical, Western tradition there has been a sea-change since the 1960s, a change even sharper than the shifting patterns of churchgoing mapped in part two. The entry of Roman Catholics into the mainstream of academic theology and the proliferation of courses in religious studies have both had a radical effect upon the study of theology within academic institutions.

Within relatively homogeneous communities, theology is typically understood as a scholarly activity undertaken by people of faith for others who share the same faith within a context of communal religious practice. Scholastic theology in medieval Europe would have been understood in this way. Anselm's celebrated depiction of theology as 'faith seeking understanding' was written in the context of a society in which 'faith', 'religion' and 'Catholicism' were all one and the same thing for his audience. In traditional Islamic societies today this is often still the dominant understanding of theology, as it remains among many communities of Orthodox Jews, traditionalist Roman Catholics and Eastern Orthodox, and amongst fundamentalist Protestants.

However, since the introduction of modern forms of theological scholarship over the last 150 years, especially within university-based theology in the West, the relationship between faith, religious practice and theology has become far more ambiguous. Furthermore, following the specific changes since the 1960s, it can no longer be assumed that all of those studying theology, or indeed all of those who teach them, within Western academic institutions share either the same faith or a common pattern of religious practice. Diversification has replaced homogeneity. Those who teach Christian theology within the academy may or may not be Christians themselves, but they certainly cannot assume today that their students are all Christians or even religiously committed at all, let alone from similar Christian denominations. As a result, a comparative rather than confessional approach to theology within the academy ensures that a variety of contrasting faith positions and religious practices are analysed critically. The theological pluralism of academia now typically reflects the cultural pluralism of Western society at large.

Yet this chapter will suggest that, even within this changing context, religious faith and practice do not simply disappear. Rather, a complex relationship between faith, practice and theology is becoming apparent in different areas of theological education within academic theology in the West.

Systematic Theology

Those who study critical theology within modern academic institutions will encounter the work of historical and present-day systematiç theology from a variety of contrasting, and sometimes competing, traditions. They will need, for example, to be as familiar with the writings of Thomas Aquinas as with those of Martin Luther and John Calvin. In the modern world they will need to study, say, both Karl Barth and Karl Rahner. As with any other arts- or social-science-based subject, it is usually considered to be inadequate to study the ideas of any single author without being able to relate those ideas critically to the competing ideas of others. Comparative, critical study is as important to systematic theology within the academy as it is to philosophy or to sociology. All three subjects can, of course, be taught in a confessional manner. At times Marxist sociology and various brands of philosophy have been taught in this way. However, the dominant approach within the Western academic institutions is either to discourage such confessional teaching, or to counter it with teaching using alternative confessional bases. Whether a critical and relatively detached approach is adopted, or a multi-confessional approach, the student is inevitably confronted in the modern academy with a self-consciously pluralistic subject.

This has a number of implications for the relationship between faith and systematic theology. Firstly, systematic theology becomes a form of history of ideas or sociology of knowledge. By juxtaposing competing understandings of theology, systematic theology becomes less the systematic exploration of the tenets of faith than a critical comparison of competing understandings of faith.[1] Indeed, few of those who teach systematic theology within the modern academy have themselves written, or will ever write, a systematic theology. Rather they are scholars who have specialized in studying the written systematic theologies of past and present theologians. They may seek to trace the provenance of these ideas, as a history-of-ideas approach does in a variety of disciplines (and most notably within philosophy). Or they may seek additional connections between these changing ideas and changes within society at large, as the sociology of knowledge attempts to do. Yet both of these approaches have a strong tendency to locate faith in a comparative and critical context ... it is the faith of others that is typically studied as much as one's own faith.

Secondly, systematic theology becomes more a comparative than a confessional form of study. Even if someone who teaches or studies theology has a strong commitment to faith and religious practice (as of course many, but not all, do), the very discipline in its modern form encourages critical comparison rather than confession. If ideas from competing theological traditions are studied in a scholarly manner, then they do need to be approached with a degree of sympathy. If they are dismissed too early, on some confessional basis, then their significance is likely to be overlooked. The careful comparison of divergent views sits uncomfortably with a mono-confessional and apologetic approach to theology.

Thirdly, the very process of modern academic theology makes it difficult to sustain an unquestioning faith. There is a clear difference between those people of faith who have never heard their faith seriously challenged and those people of faith

---

[1] Daphne Hampson's *Christian Contradictions: The Structures of Lutheran and Catholic Thought* (Cambridge: Cambridge University Press, 2001) provides a striking example of how this can still be done by someone writing as a post-Christian theologian.

who retain their faith in the context of a pluralistic and critical academy. This remains the case even when the content of the two faiths appears to be identical. For example, people from these two contexts may have a similar belief in a personal God. Yet those in the pluralistic context are aware that this belief is challenged by many other people on a variety of grounds, whereas those in the first context are not. The faith of those in the pluralistic context is no longer an unquestioning faith: it is a faith held in contrast to (and sometimes in defiance of) others in society.

It would, though, be a mistake to assume from this that faith has little to do with systematic theology in modern academic institutions. Many, perhaps most, of those who actually write a systematic theology in the first place do have an explicit faith commitment located within a specific community of religious practice. It is clearly incumbent, then, on those studying a particular systematic theology to seek to understand that faith commitment – whether they share that commitment themselves or not. Again, many (but not all) students of systematic theology are drawn into the discipline precisely because they have a sense of 'faith seeking understanding'. Just as many students of philosophy or the social sciences have a personal interest in their subject, so do many students of systematic theology. More than that, some people come to systematic theology because they are convinced that a mature faith needs a comparative and critical assessment. Systematic theology thus allows them to compare and contrast their own faith with that of others and, in the process, to refine and nuance their faith.

Religious Studies

A further process of refinement is possible for those who are prepared to compare and contrast their own faith with that of non-Christian religious traditions. Sometimes termed comparative theology (rather than what was once termed 'comparative religion'), Christian theology is set within a broader context of, say, Jewish theology or Islamic theology, in an attempt to identify and perhaps evaluate points of convergence and divergence.

Such an approach is not without its critics. Some, following Karl Barth, would reject it on the grounds that Christianity is not 'a religion'. The uniqueness of Christian faith means that it is always mistaken to compare it with any other so-called 'faith', whether this faith is a secular form of 'faith' or one drawn from one or other of the world religions. On this understanding, Christian faith is wholly incomparable, so any attempt at such comparison inevitably involves serious distortion. Christian faith is based solely upon the Word of God made known uniquely in Jesus Christ, not upon some shared religious experience common to humanity or upon some knowledge of God derived independently of Jesus Christ.

In contrast, some within the academic discipline of religious studies argue that comparative theology is mistaken because it is too fideistic. They argue that religious studies differs from comparative theology in that it is 'value-free' and independent of any faith commitment. So, whereas comparative theology, or traditional theology in any form, is viewed primarily in confessional terms, religious studies is seen as a detached, scientific discipline concerned with describing and analysing religious phenomena without any existential commitment to them. The very term 'religious studies' rather than 'comparative religion' is often preferred for this reason: the latter is considered to be too value-laden and judgemental. On this understanding, theology in any form is a discipline suitable particularly for those training for ministry within churches, whereas religious studies is a discipline more suitable for those training to be teachers in a non-confessional setting. Or, to express this differently, theology aims to promote and refine faith whereas religious studies seeks rather to promote greater knowledge and discernment about religious issues. Theology is thus a fideistic discipline suitable for ministers, whereas religious studies is a detached discipline suitable for diplomats or civil servants.

It is not too difficult to show that both of these criticisms hardly match the disciplines of theology and religious studies as they are now typically taught and studied in the West. In their different ways they present caricatures of both theology and religious studies.

In the light of the understanding of systematic theology already outlined it is difficult to maintain the sharp contrast between theology and religious studies in the second criticism. It is simply not the case in Western academic institutions that theology is invariably a confessional discipline taught in faith to people who share that faith. Even those training for ordained ministry in many mainstream denominations will be expected to study a wide variety of approaches to theology which they do not personally share. It is also misleading to imagine that all of those studying religious studies have no prior religious commitments and approach their subject in a detached rather than fideistic manner. On the contrary, many are likely to engage in religious studies precisely because of their existential interests and concerns. It is quite possible for those, say, with defined Christian commitments themselves to wish to relate these commitments to those within religious traditions outside Christianity. Some distinguished Jewish and Islamic scholars have chosen to study Christian theology for similar reasons. A desire to study differing religious traditions does not in itself exclude a commitment to a particular tradition. Indeed, as with the study of art or music, those who study a particular subject might typically be expected to have a strong attachment to at least some aspects of that subject. Religious studies, in practice, often has a very similar balance of faith and critical detachment to theology as it is typically taught and studied today in the West.

The first criticism, based upon the dogmatic claim that Christian theology is wholly incomparable, ignores the considerable body of scholarship that has been concerned to analyse the Jewish, Roman and Greek roots of Christian theology. It also ignores the family relationship of Christianity to Islam and the fact that the Koran itself contains sacred traditions about Jesus Christ. The relationship between Judaism and Christianity has received particular attention in Western academic research. In part this has been stimulated by the growing awareness that some forms of Christianity have acted historically as bearers of anti-Judaism and may even have contributed to the culture of European anti-Semitism that made possible the horrors of the Jewish Holocaust. However, it has also been stimulated by Jewish and Christian theologians reading each others' works and sometimes training and studying together. Such study reveals the extent to which early Christianity derived much from Judaism and still shares many theological precepts today.

Some scholars have also studied the extent to which early Christianity borrowed concepts more widely from the Mediterranean world. For example, the New Testament scholar Wayne Meeks has argued at length that the Pauline virtues have much in common with contemporary Graeco-Roman virtues.[2] Or, to take a later example, Augustine in the fourth century consciously borrowed from Cicero in his understanding of both natural law and just-war theory. In turn, Aquinas was later to borrow directly from the newly rediscovered ideas of Aristotle (preserved, ironically, by Islamic scholars) in writing his own systematic theology.

None of this contradicts the distinctiveness or uniqueness of Christian theology, or specifically its central focus upon Jesus Christ, yet it does question the claim that Christian theology is wholly incomparable. On the basis of this considerable amount of modern scholarship, there do seem to be solid grounds for the claim instead that Christian faith does have a clear relationship with other forms of theistic faith outside Christianity.

But what about those forms of faith that are not theistic? Theologians again soon divide on this question. As noted in the first chapter, a theologian such as Hans Küng argues that on the global issues of international peace or the environment there are points of contact across many different forms of religious faith – whether theistic or not – and that such issues require us urgently to recognize these.[3] Others, however, remain unconvinced, arguing that attempts to supply a comprehensive definition of 'religious faith' have been remarkably unsuccessful. Whatever the outcome of this debate, it is difficult to maintain convincingly that Christian faith, let alone Christian practice, is wholly incomparable. Both systematic theology and religious studies in the Western academic institutions have a similar tension or paradox. On the one hand, those who study and teach in these areas still show considerable evidence of faith and religious practice. Yet, on the other, they also seem to value critical detachment.

---

[2] Wayne A. Meeks, *The Origins of Christian Morality* (New Haven: Yale University Press, 1993).

[3] Hans Küng, *A Global Ethic for Global Politics and Economics* (London: SCM Press, 1997).

Biblical Studies

It might be supposed that such tension is largely absent from biblical studies. Indeed, an outsider might be forgiven for assuming that nobody would spend his or her life studying Christian Scriptures unless s/he was personally committed to those Scriptures and believed that they contained the key to salvation. Yet, in practice, there is as much tension here as in any other area of theology or religious studies in the Western academia. Many biblical scholars do indeed approach their subject from a perspective of faith and religious practice, but some do not. And even among those who do, they hold many different opinions on the authority of Scripture in relation to their faith and religious practice. Pluralism and tension abound here as well.

At some levels, this is hardly surprising. There are many technical aspects of biblical studies, such as the linguistic, source and textual areas, which require considerable skills but not faith as such. So, just as many classical scholars can derive pleasure and satisfaction from studying texts that are at variance with their own beliefs and commitments, it is not difficult to see how some secular scholars can approach biblical texts in a similar way. In both contexts there are intellectual challenges and puzzles that can fully engage the imaginations of those with the appropriate skills, but without involving any existential commitment on their part. Establishing the chronological order of the Synoptic Gospels, say, arguing in detail for or against the existence of Q, or recovering the most reliable Greek text of the New Testament, are not activities in themselves that require Christian faith. It might even be argued that such study can sharpen skills that can then be applied to other more pragmatic areas of life. Ironically, such an argument was used at the beginning of the twentieth century for the training of Anglican ordinands: typically they (and many other intellectuals) were required to study classics rather than theology as their training for ministry. Perhaps there was even a presumption that studying a work such as Plato's *Republic* (a particular favourite for that generation) improved the minds of ordinands rather more than studying the Bible.

By the middle of the twentieth century, Anglican ordination training had changed very considerably. Now it was assumed, and not just by Anglican evangelicals, that a rigorous study of biblical exegesis was an essential part of ordination training. Yet, after a century of biblical criticism, the dominant assumption was that biblical exegesis must be conducted in a critical context – especially that of historical criticism. Nonetheless, biblical exegesis for Anglican ordinands of all descriptions was a confessional activity. It was studied to inform the future teaching and preaching ministry of these ordinands, who themselves constituted the majority of those studying theology at English universities (in Scotland there was a very similar pattern of male, Presbyterian ordinands forming the majority of those studying theology at Edinburgh, Glasgow, St Andrews or Aberdeen).

However, since the 1960s Western academic institutions have been radically transformed. In Britain (as elsewhere in Europe and North America) a majority of those studying theology in university are neither male nor ordinands and are not necessarily Anglicans (or, in Scotland, Presbyterians) at all. And biblical interpretation has assumed at least as large a role as biblical exegesis in the syllabus. As a result this syllabus can no longer presume that the function of biblical studies is to inform the teaching and preaching of (male) Anglican or Presbyterian ordinands. Such a confessional function has been replaced with a more comparative function. The syllabus in biblical studies is now more likely to require students to become familiar with different and contrasting patterns of hermeneutics. Biblical interpretation requires an awareness that across time and across different contemporary cultures (diachronically and synchronically) biblical texts are understood, interpreted and appropriated very differently. Pluralism and comparative critical study have once again entered the discipline. Biblical interpretation involves the exploration of different and sometimes contradictory faith communities as they have sought to use the Bible. As a result, this new discipline raises many similar issues to those raised by systematic theology.

Church History

The changed constituency of Western academic institutions has also had a radical effect upon the teaching of church history. In a mono-confessional context church history is typically interpreted in the light of particular denominations. Anglicans pay particular attention to Anglican divines such as Hooker, Presbyterians to Knox, Methodists to Wesley, and so forth. Church history is thus focused upon those people or events considered most significant to that faith community. More polemically, this focus is sometimes portrayed as the path of 'orthodoxy' to be contrasted with the errors propagated by other Christians. As a result, church history in such mono-confessional contexts constitutes an important feature of identity, reinforcing boundaries between faithful Christians and others.

In a pluralist environment, church history becomes more complicated. It is not, of course, value free: particular people and events are still selected for discussion and others are not; those selected are given different amounts of time and consideration; and the perspectives of different historians inevitably shape their interpretations of the significance of these people and events. Once it is conceded that selection and interpretation are inextricably involved in any study of history, and especially in any study of church history, then absolute detachment is no more possible (or perhaps even desirable) here than it is in religious studies. Even within the pluralist context of the West today, faith, or rather a multiplicity of faiths, is still a part of church history.

However, the multiplicity of faiths involved in church history today does entail a greater attention than in the past to divergent branches of Christianity set in a variety of cultures. Any serious study of church history pays attention not simply to Western Christianity but also to Christianity in non-Western countries (as the second and third case-studies in the previous chapter attempted to do). The history of Christian missions, for example, is not simply relegated to a separate discipline of mission studies, but is part of a global account of Christian history. In addition, sociological studies of new religious movements, cults and sects in both the West and non-Western countries form a part of this global account. And, within accounts of early Christianity, previously discredited movements such as that of Gnosticism are treated with a new seriousness. Christian history is depicted less as the history of the successful 'orthodox' and more as a varied and pluriform family of interrelated movements arising from the New Testament.

Christian Ethics

Very similar changes can also be found in Christian ethics. A changing constituency within the Western academic world, allied to a shift towards hermeneutics, has radically changed the discipline. However, in this instance, the current dominance of virtue ethics presents a particularly intricate intertwining of faith, practice and theology – an intertwining which characterizes applied theology in general.

A generation ago, when university theological students were predominantly young male ordinands, Christian ethics (if it was taught at all in Britain) was distinctly more confessional in character than it is today. Classic Anglican moral theologians of the first half of the twentieth century, such as Kenneth Kirk and Robert Mortimer (both later to become bishops), presented a mixture of ethical/theological analysis and advice on pastoral practice in their books. They could assume that their audience of ordinands shared the same faith and religious practices as themselves and were looking to be guided about how they should respond to ethical issues once they were themselves ordained. Similarly Roman Catholic moral theologians of the time, or Church of Scotland practical theologians north of the Border, also mixed analysis and pastoral advice in their work, assuming that they wrote from faith to faith within their respective communities. As a result, Catholic moral theologians of this period largely ignored Luther and Calvin, just as Scottish practical theologians paid little attention to Aquinas. Christian ethics at the time was predominantly confessional, both in its scope and in its approach. That is, it was written from within particular denominations by people of particular faith traditions to fellow believers.

Within Western academic institutions such an approach would be less likely to commend itself today. An approach to Christian ethics that simply bypassed one of the major traditions would usually be judged to be inadequate. The entry of Catholic theologians into the mainstream of the Western academy has ensured that the natural law tradition is taken seriously even within formerly Presbyterian or Anglican faculties. In turn, these Catholic theologians have taken seriously the biblical scholarship generated by generations of Reformed and Anglican theologians. This two-way process has ensured that Christian ethics is now more genuinely ecumenical than it typically was a generation ago. Scholars across denominations and across different faith traditions mutually read each other's works. They may still disagree with each other – ecumenical dialogue does not guarantee consensus – but they are less likely than hitherto simply to ignore each other.

This shift within the academic study of Christian ethics entails changes similar to those already noted in other areas of theology: critical comparison tends to replace a mono-confessional approach; pluralism rather than consensus predominates; and a degree of academic detachment becomes evident. There is no need to rehearse these points again within this new context.

However, there is one point that is new here. A multi-confessional approach to Christian ethics soon reveals that there are incommensurable moral differences between Christians (as part one of this book has shown). Of course, there always were real moral differences between Christians within particular denominations. Nevertheless, as long as Christian ethics was conducted separately by denominations, each might maintain the hope that their internal moral differences could in time be resolved. The doctrine of the 'consensus of the faithful' reinforced this hope. However, once Christian ethics is studied in a multi-confessional and ecumenical context, then it soon becomes apparent that such differences are in reality incommensurable. For example, there is no way finally to resolve crucial differences between denominations about when full human life begins or when, if ever, it is legitimate to end human life. As a result, bioethics and just-war ethics have both faced differences between Christians, which a comparative, critical approach to Christian ethics can help us better to understand but not to resolve. More than that, such an approach has revealed that there are sometimes stronger connections on particular moral issues between Christians and their secular counterparts than there are between opposing Christians.

The current debates about stem-cell research or physician-assisted suicide demonstrate this clearly. Supporters and opponents of stem-cell research using embryos created by cell nuclear replacement can be found among both Christians and secularists. Within particular denominations it can, of course, be maintained that only one side represents 'orthodoxy' from a Christian perspective. Traditionalist Roman Catholics have indeed held this view, condemning such stem-cell research as contrary to natural law and to the gospel. Yet across denominations, such claims to 'orthodoxy' soon appear tendentious where there is no agreement about when full human life begins, or indeed whether an embryo created by cell nuclear replacement constitutes a potential human being at all. Even physician-assisted suicide, which is rejected by most denominations, is not condemned by all theologians.[4] The latter tend to argue that it is too readily concluded from the doctrines of creation and resurrection that physician-assisted suicide is wrong. In contrast, they maintain that a belief in a life beyond this life might actually encourage Christians to believe that there is no need to cling to this life. My point is not to side here with either position but merely to illustrate that a critical comparative approach to Christian ethics soon reveals incommensurable differences of faith and practice between Christians on moral issues.

Given this, a shift away from ethical decision making within academic Christian ethics and towards virtue ethics is hardly surprising. As a result of this shift, recent Christian ethics has rediscovered new links with systematic theology and, ironically, with sociology. Within virtue ethics, the focus is upon virtuous character and upon those communities that nurture and shape character. We are the products less of rational, individualistic moral decisions made from one situation to another than of ways of living shaped by tradition and community. As Christians, our moral lives and characters are shaped by the faith and practice of worshipping communities and the traditions that they carry over across the centuries.[5] Such an understanding of Christian ethics places it firmly within the broader context of applied or practical theology.

---

[4] See, for example, Paul Badham in my *Euthanasia and the Churches* (London: Cassell, 1998).
[5] See further my *Churchgoing and Christian Ethics* (Cambridge: Cambridge University Press, 1999).

Applied Theology

Applied or practical theology within Western academic institutions is the discipline especially concerned with this interaction between faith and practice. Sometimes this relationship is envisaged as faith shaping practice, sometimes as practice shaping faith, and sometimes as an interaction of the two. Applied theology has a similar comparative, critical role to that of systematic theology as well as having clear links to secular disciplines such as sociology. A discipline that was once considered to be an appendix to systematic and biblical theology within academic institutions, has now become a central player in understanding the tension or, perhaps better, interaction between faith and practice evident in all of the other areas of theology. It is also a discipline that has made considerable use of the social sciences to understand this interaction more fully.

Applied theology a generation ago often consisted of little more than practical advice to ordinands. A teacher with considerable experience of ordained ministry would teach young ordinands how they should conduct funeral services, how they should preach, how they should conduct pastoral visiting, or similar related tasks. Having studied biblical and systematic theology, the applied or practical theologian was the person responsible for teaching ordinands the practicalities of ordained ministry. In the Church of Scotland applied theologians typically taught within a university, but often had been university chaplains or highly regarded parish ministers first. In the Church of England 'pastoral theology' (as it was usually termed) was more typically taught within a seminary, albeit by priests of similar pastoral experience to their counterparts in Scotland.

However well intended this model of applied theology, it faced serious difficulties. The parish experience of those teaching applied theology for any length of time, whether in the university or in a seminary, inevitably became more distant. So, just as trainee teachers frequently resent being told how to teach children by those who no longer teach them themselves, ordinands were often suspicious of the advice they were being given by former parish ministers, however experienced they had once been. Again, models of professional formation from disciplines such as medicine suggested that the proper place for practical training is not in an academic institution but in the context of the job itself. Critical placements alongside reflexive practitioners were more likely to generate good professional formation.

Once the profile of those studying theology also changed it was soon clear that this 'hints and tips for ordinands' approach to applied theology was no longer appropriate. The pluralism of present-day students within the Western academy, noted already in all other areas of theology, has also had a radical impact upon academic applied theology. The discipline still maintained a central focus upon faith and practice, but it could no longer assume any shared faith or practice among theological students. The relationship between divergent, and sometimes conflicting, patterns of Christian faith and practice now became the primary subject matter of applied theology within academic institutions. The next chapter will look at four recent examples of this new genre of applied theology.

The concept of 'praxis' is sometimes used within applied theology to denote this new understanding. Initially taken from Marxist studies, it suggests that behaviour is given priority over theory, but that there is still a constant interaction between the two. In a more traditional understanding of religious practice it was often assumed that faith takes priority over practice. Christian faith thus sets the template for Christian practice. Within theological studies it was frequently assumed that the primary task of theology was to establish an adequate faith based upon a careful study of the Bible and Christian tradition. Once that had been achieved, then issues of practice could be addressed. In a similar way it was often assumed in philosophy that the primary task was to produce clarity of thought and theory before any practical problems could be adequately addressed. Marxist studies reversed this understanding, arguing that what people actually do and how they behave should be the starting point for analysis. On this approach, practice is given priority and theory is, in the first place, the attempt to understand practice. Once theory is adequately grounded in an analysis of present-day practice then it too can shape future practice.

By no means all applied theologians give explicit credence to Marxism (although some liberation theologians certainly do), but they do typically work from this approach based upon praxis. In the relationship between faith and practice, they give far more attention to practice than most other theologians do. Those working within applied liturgical studies often argue that it is worship that shapes doctrine and in turn is shaped by doctrine. Those working within Christian ethics argue that it is Christian communities that mould Christian character, which, in turn, shapes the ethical decision making of individuals. Those working in Christian education argue that Christian formation within families, churches and, perhaps, within schools, is crucial for nurturing faith, and that this faith, once nurtured, should then inform Christian formation. In each of these areas within applied theology there is a priority given to practice, as well as an awareness of a continuing interaction between practice and faith. And in each of these areas the social sciences assume an important role.

Naturally, an extensive use of social sciences within any area of theology is likely to generate suspicions of relativism and reductionism. A suspicion of relativism is raised here, as it is in other areas of theology, by the increasing pluralism of those teaching and studying applied theology. And a suspicion of reductionism is generated by the fear that extensive use of social sciences will soon eliminate transcendence altogether. Churches and church practices will soon, so it is feared, be reduced to the purely secular. An example of this fear has already been noted in the previous chapter in reaction to socio-logical interpretations of changing patterns of church membership in South Korea. Similarly, the use of organiz-ational or business theory to understand churches is often condemned by theologians as reducing churches to nothing more than secular organizations or (worse still) businesses.

This is surely a profound misunderstanding of both applied theology and the social sciences. To explain or understand churches or religious practice in social scientific terms is not in itself to explain them away (as the final chapter will argue in relation to David Martin's work). There manifestly are, for example, financial and economic features of institutional churches: they have budgets, they raise income and they spend money. All of these features can be compared with the similar activities of secular organizations and, if they are to be achieved effectively and efficiently, might benefit from such comparison.

But to assume from this that institutional churches are 'nothing but' financial/economic institutions would be very misguided. Similarly, church leadership does have points in common with other forms of secular leadership. Yet studying it in this way does not of itself imply that it is *only* to be understood in this way. A judicious use of social science within applied theology is perfectly compatible with a commitment to transcendence.

At the heart of applied theology, then, is a concern for faith, practice and theology. Even if the relationship between these three has become more complex and varied within Western academic institutions today, a concern to study and better to understand their relationship remains.

9

Changes in Applied Theology

The previous chapter has mapped broad changes that have taken place in academic theology since the 1960s. The present chapter will focus very specifically upon these changes within current applied theology in Britain, using four recent books to illustrate them.

The radical change of direction started in the late 1960s and early 1970s by Bob Lambourne and then Michael Wilson at Birmingham University, by Jim Blackie and his successor Duncan Forrester at Edinburgh University, and by James Whyte at St Andrews University, has continued to influence applied theology in Britain. Under their direction, applied theology in Britain has become emphatically ecumenical, open to serious insights from the social sciences, and established as a more central theological discipline than in the past. The sort of 'hints and tips for ordinands' approach, outlined in the previous chapter, has given way to a more professional and rigorous discipline which has spread into other universities and colleges during the 1980s and 1990s. Under the influence of this new approach there has been a flourishing of applied theology literature within Britain.

I have chosen four recent books, all published within a year of each other, to represent the best of this literature in Britain. In order of their publication, they are: Elaine L. Graham's *Transforming Practice: Pastoral Theology in an Age of Uncertainty*,[1] Paul Ballard and John Pritchard's *Practical Theology in Action: Christian Thinking in the Service of Church and Society*,[2] Wesley Carr's *Handbook of Pastoral Studies: Learning and Practising Christian Ministry*,[3] and Emmanuel Y. Lartey's *In Living Colour:*

---

[1] London: Mowbray, 1996.
[2] London: SPCK, 1996.
[3] London: SPCK, 1997.

An Intercultural Approach to Pastoral Care and Counselling.[4] Rather than reviewing their contents point by point, this chapter will seek to compare and contrast them, albeit using a variety of criteria.

What criteria might be suggested for assessing the relative merits of applied theology? An obvious one is competence. Fortunately, the authors are very competent and thoroughly familiar with the changes in applied theology in Britain. Although counselling has remained an important ingredient in traditional forms of applied theology, it has never been as dominant as it was in the United States in the 1960s. The warnings of Bob Lambourne to take the social and contextual features of applied theology seriously have long been heeded in Britain. In the 1980s, the work of Alastair Campbell, especially his *Rediscovering Pastoral Care,*[5] and the work of his former student Stephen Pattison, especially his *A Critique of Pastoral Care,*[6] drew greater attention in the discipline to the specifically theological resources within Christian communities. In the 1990s, hermeneutics became ever more important – a perspective again set out intelligently in Stephen Pattison's *Pastoral Care and Liberation Theology.*[7] All four books under comparison here are well aware of these changes in applied theology and act as reliable guides to those less familiar with them.

Another criterion might be scope. Unfortunately, this raises an obvious problem; despite much argument, theologians have been unable to agree even about a title for the discipline. In this book I have opted for the generic title 'applied theology'. However, Elaine Graham prefers the title 'pastoral theology', Wesley Carr 'pastoral studies', Emmanuel Lartey 'pastoral care and counselling' and Paul Ballard and John Pritchard 'practical theology'. Doubtless there are some different emphases reflected in these choices – for example, some authors, such as Emmanuel Lartey, are more interested in counselling than, for example, Elaine Graham. Moreover, some

[4] London: Cassell, 1997.
[5] London: SPCK, 1981.
[6] London: SPCK, 1988.
[7] Cambridge: Cambridge University Press, 1994.

authors, such as Paul Ballard and John Pritchard, relate the discipline more tightly to the churches than others (albeit remaining well aware of pluralism within these churches). These are real differences and some seek to distinguish the various terms they use on the basis of these, but the exercise is frankly less than convincing. Just as attempts to distinguish between 'morality' and 'ethics' usually end in intellectual confusion (their different origins in Latin and Greek respectively are surely their most notable difference), there are obvious overlaps in the actual areas of interest discussed by all four authors, whatever label they choose. Perhaps it is best to consider this as simply an issue of personal preference.

A more serious criterion is new perspectives. Which of the four books offers new perspectives that might shape the future direction of applied theology in Britain? Here I believe that Elaine Graham and Emmanuel Lartey are the winners. Both bring distinctive perspectives to the discipline, which challenge many present assumptions. For Elaine Graham it is insights from feminism that she believes need to be integrated better into applied theology, whereas for Emmanuel Lartey it is ethnicity and culture.

Elaine Graham, now professor in social and pastoral theology at Manchester University, has already argued for a distinctively feminist perspective in her earlier writings. In *Transforming Practice* she argues that the shift from an individualistic to a more communal approach to applied theology can be seen, at least in part, as a shift from modernity to postmodernity. For her:

> Postmodern perspectives portray the self as a subject-in-relation, whose identity is forged within the complex interplay of economic, cultural and political factors. Contemporary pastoral/practical theology is gradually revising its own implicit ideals of the person to encompass such contexts.[8]

She believes that feminism can help to transform the discipline still further in this direction. Her specific contribution is to take the familiar feminist critiques of patriarchy in society, in the

---

[8] Graham, *Transforming Practice*, p. 51.

Church and in the Bible and Christian tradition, and to relate these to the discipline of applied theology in Britain. She believes that feminist transforming practice can help faith communities to 'revision' their theological horizons.

Emmanuel Lartey, then lecturer in pastoral studies and pastoral theology at Birmingham University, shares this contextual approach to applied theology. His distinctive contribution is to direct attention to the complexities produced by radically different cultures interacting. He uses his own unique experience of British culture, African culture and British-African culture effectively in his challenge to applied theology. The approach that he takes follows the changes that he identifies taking place in the four-yearly International Congress of Pastoral Care and Counselling. The first meeting was at Edinburgh in 1979 on the theme 'The Risks of Freedom' – a conference that took seriously the need for a social perspective in Christian applied theology. The fifth International Congress was in Toronto in 1995 on the theme 'Babylon and Jerusalem: Stories of Transition in a Strange Land'. At this, Christianity was only one amongst several religious traditions being considered. The discipline had become interreligious as well as intercultural. Emmanuel Lartey broadly welcomes this change:

> This congress sought to move the movement on into the reality of pluralism in the religious and cultural contexts in which pastoral care and counselling is engaged with the world today and to face pastoral practitioners with the ambiguities and difficulties in communication, and of learning, method and culture in the practice of pastoral care and counselling.[9]

This raises a very interesting problem. The rich variety of perspectives and hermeneutics offered by both Elaine Graham and Emmanuel Lartey undoubtedly make applied theology more complex and intellectually interesting along the lines discussed in the previous chapter. Yet do they also make it unusable in practice? Applied theology is no longer just concerned with people who have 'pastoral problems', but with all of us; it is not just concerned with individuals as individuals,

---

[9] Lartey, *In Living Colour*, p. 28.

but also with communities and, indeed, with wide-ranging social and political structures. Applied theology cannot rely any more upon a single approach to theology or the Bible, but must use several (potentially conflicting) approaches; it is no longer confined to a single culture, but relates to many different cultures and sub-cultures and to the interactions between them; it is not even confined to Christianity any longer, but relates to many different religious and 'spiritual' traditions. In short, applied theology may have become so ambitious and diffuse that it is in real danger of lacking focus and practical value. Emmanuel Lartey offers a number of helpful paths and diagrams to guide readers through these confusing ambiguities and complexities confronting students in applied theology today. Nevertheless, by including so much, insights might be dissipated and perspectives may become blurred.

Another criterion is accessibility. The most accessible of the four books here is *Practical Theology in Action* by Paul Ballard, senior lecturer in practical theology at University of Wales, Cardiff, and John Pritchard, then Archdeacon of Canterbury. The book has cheerful cartoons on the cover, is reasonably priced and makes theories palatable by relating them to fictional people ... Sheila, Bill, Sarah, Charles and others. As the most church-based of the books, it is also the one that comes closest to the old 'hints and tips' approach. It is written with splendid clarity and is undoubtedly popular amongst those theological college students who are irritated by technical theology. The authors' intentions are clear on all of this and they would be the first to admit that this is not a book intended for professional theologians. It would be quite wrong to judge it as such. However, what can be asked here is whether or not Paul Ballard and John Pritchard succeed in one of their most central claims, namely to show that the pastoral cycle provides a way of unifying the different approaches and perspectives in applied theology. Four broad approaches are identified: applied theology understood as the application of biblical/theological principles to practical situations; correlation understood as the setting of insights from theological and cultural/social scientific disciplines alongside each other; praxis understood as theory and practice mutually informing each other; and habitus understood as developing communities of faith that shape Christian lives. Each of these four approaches can indeed be adopted as different forms of theological reflection within the pastoral cycle. Yet what if they conflict? How are tensions between them to be resolved? There are obvious points of conflict between the first and second approaches and, in practice, between them and the fourth. And exponents of radical forms of praxis theology are often impatient of the 'gradualism' of other approaches. In their admirable concern to offer a clear and smooth account of these different approaches, Paul Ballard and John Pritchard may well underplay these conflicts within applied theology.

The fourth book, *Handbook of Pastoral Studies*, by Wesley Carr, now Dean of Westminster Abbey, provides an alternative approach. His earlier books in this area – *The Priestlike Task, The Pastor as Theologian, Ministry and the Media, Manifold Wisdom* and *Brief Encounters*[10] – are all much used within pastoral theology. SPCK's series *New Library of Pastoral Care*, which he has done much to shape, has also been a major influence within the discipline. *Handbook of Pastoral Studies* acts as a useful overview of both the series and Wesley Carr's own work. It is rather longer and somewhat more demanding than *Practical Theology in Action* and, in style, it is not so didactic or so worried about smoothing over conflicts. Wesley Carr acknowledges frankly the difficulties of accepting and articulating Christian belief today and the challenges of pluralism and 'common religion'. Writing before his historic role in the funeral of Princess Diana, he perceptively notes developing rituals (such as laying flowers in public places after a car accident) and the need for church ministers to be sensitive to them. He sets out, in a fairly descriptive manner, differing approaches to applied theology based variously upon psychology and sociology and sees the small-group theory of Bion as a useful bridge for the discipline:

> It would be naive to suggest that Bion's theory of the individual, the group, society, basic assumptions and work groups and its elaboration magically solves such problems ... Yet pastors need a working framework by which to hold together as best they may the disparate aspects of their activity. These ideas ... draw attention to the way that every

[10] London: SPCK, 1985, 1989, 1990, 1991 and 1995 respectively.

human being lives within a set of human institutions which can each be thought of in a systemic fashion.[11]

Wesley Carr offers the student a broad map, with some hints along the way, but expects each to decide her or his own path. Even his definition of theology is broad and open-ended: 'theological reflection is a constructed, ordered, reflective enquiry on the interaction of one's self (person and role) and one's context (God, the world and the neighbour) which produces a conceptual framework which leads to action'.[12] In contrast to the other three books, Wesley Carr is more concerned to supply a critical overview of applied theology than to prescribe a specific approach or path within it.

Which of these four books should finally be recommended to students? Of course, much depends upon the context and level of the students themselves. If they are beginning their studies, then perhaps they could cope with Wesley Carr's book. It is somewhat long-winded in places, but it should allow them to think for themselves and to grow within the discipline. If, however, the students are a little more advanced, then the choice is perhaps between Elaine Graham and Emmanuel Lartey. Assuming that they had already read some feminist theology, they may not learn anything very startling from Elaine Graham. She writes well and thoughtfully, but it is not too difficult to anticipate her conclusions. Emmanuel Lartey, in contrast, strikingly and uniquely illustrates the changes in theological education mapped in the previous chapter. His writing can be a little pedestrian in places and his chapters are uneven in length and content. Nevertheless, this is the book that finally made me think. He raises very serious intercultural problems within applied theology in Britain today that are still largely unexplored. In the context of *Changing Worlds* he left me more confused but nonetheless stimulated than when I started to read his book.

In the 1950s, Teilhard de Chardin memorably characterized evolution as increasing complexification with convergent integration. Within applied theology today, Emmanuel Lartey

---

[11] Carr, *Handbook of Pastoral Studies*, p. 91.
[12] Carr, *Handbook of Pastoral Studies*, p. 118

adds uniquely to increasing complexification. However, the task of any convergent theological integration (or, indeed, convergent integration within physical evolution) may yet be beyond the horizon of *Changing Worlds*.

10

Sociology and Theology

Throughout *Changing Worlds*, sociological and theological methods have been used in the belief that both are essential for theological realism. In Britain the single most important influence in this area has been David Martin. In 1996 he published his mature collection *Reflections on Sociology and Theology*[1] which brings together different aspects of the theological/sociological research that he has been doing for over thirty years. This final chapter will compare this work with some of his earlier writings.

The influence of David Martin on British sociology of religion as a whole has been immense. Together with Bryan Wilson he has taught, examined and encouraged a generation of us currently involved in the discipline. However, unlike Wilson, he has maintained an interest in theology. After years of teaching at the London School of Economics, he was finally ordained, continuing an active ministry at Guildford Cathedral since his retirement. For those who know his other writings, the 1996 collection of essays on sociology and theology will come as little surprise. Like most of his works, the predominant mode of the essays here is sociological, yet underlying them are a number of implicit, and sometimes explicit, theological commitments. As always, his essays are multi-layered, creative and, in places, elusive.

Throughout his writings there is an implicit, and sometimes explicit, tension between the different worlds that he inhabits. Writing three decades earlier in the Preface and Acknowledgements of his highly influential *A Sociology of English Religion*,[2] he notes his own differences from sociologists such as Wilson and

---

[1] David Martin, *Reflections on Sociology and Theology* (Oxford: Clarendon Press, 1996).

[2] David Martin, *A Sociology of English Religion* (London: SCM Press, 1967).

156

theologians such as John Robinson or Harvey Cox writing on the issue of secularization. Yet he concludes:

> ... our perspectives must above all be realistic: to take but one example we need to be realistic when we consider ecumenical aspiration in relation to social fissures of nation, colour and status, and to the fundamental and very varied types of religious organization which had found constricted and creative lodgement within them. Theological discussion (like political discussion) must generally take place on a level of high-flown and self-deluding linguistic camouflage. Nevertheless the key word of recent debates has been honesty, and if we are to have the honesty about the Church – that 'wonderful and sacred mystery' as the prayer book very properly calls it – then sociological perspectives and research are not a marginal luxury but an essential.[3]

What is remarkable about this passage is just how many of its ideas are still present a generation later in *Reflections*: his suspicion of easy sentiments about ecumenism (despite his own long-standing ecumenical friendships); his awareness of social fissures in religious organizations; his comparison of theological and political forms of discourse; his isolation of key signs and metaphors (here, it is that of honesty); his love of the language and resonances of the 1662 prayer book (in which he had been nourished even as a Methodist child); and his insistence, albeit against the odds, that sociological perspectives are essential to an adequate theological understanding of the Church. There is also another feature that soon follows this quotation, namely his wit in a context of dissonance. It is worth also quoting the following splendid passage in full:

> My major personal debt is to my wife, who has heard it all before and who tried to prevent me from indulging prejudice more than was necessary for my psychological well-being. The liveliness and acerbity of those prejudices may suggest another debt. A pigeon put among the cats is not in a position of maximum security. The London School of Economics is hardly renowned for piety, and a believer

[3] Martin, *A Sociology*, pp. 11–12.

working with a noble company of 'cultured despisers' needs frequently to remind himself that faith, in Luther's and Kierkegaard's sense, involves a vigorous scepticism not only about the Church but about all those quasi-religious props that contemporary men (cultured and otherwise) use to maintain their sanity – occasionally with regrettable success.[4]

I suspect that many of us have longed to be able to write like that. Like the man himself, the emotions keep switching from one sentence to the next – love for a woman, an awareness of strong and determined beliefs, a concern about health, a gentle humility, a personal piety and scepticism competing with each other, and a strong sense of human foibles. Then there is the unforgettable image of David as the pigeon amongst all those well-armed Goliath LSE cats. Next there is the curious theological combination of Luther and Kierkegaard – surely intentional and thought provoking. At their best, David Martin's sentences contain paradoxes, binary oppositions (a favourite device of his) and quirky associations that repay reading and rereading, even after many years.

At the heart of Martin's *Reflections,* as in his earlier work, is a conviction that sociology and theology share a number of characteristics, of which three are particularly important: both disciplines are pattern-seeking forms of enquiry; both return constantly to seminal thinkers; and both depend heavily upon metaphors. The first and third of these characteristics are shared with a number of areas of physical science – notably modern physics at both quantum and cosmological levels – but the second is not. Whereas most forms of physical science keep moving forward, seldom showing much interest, except for historical purposes, in their forebears, sociologists and theologians are profoundly retrospective. Within the sociology of religion, the works of Weber and Durkheim (and Marx for more radical forms of sociology) are subject to constant examination and re-examination in a manner very similar to the work of theologians. In both disciplines, pattern-seeking and metaphors are constantly tested and retested against the ideas of seminal thinkers. Of course the theologian, like

[4] Martin, *A Sociology,* pp. 13–14.

the philosopher, draws upon many more seminal thinkers over a much greater length of time than the sociologist. Moreover, the theologian tends to write *sub specie aeternitatis*, whereas the sociologist, if not the philosopher, remains firmly terrestrial. Nevertheless they are, so David Martin argues, involved in parallel forms of undertaking, which intersect at points of conflict and change.

Perhaps the place where he expresses this most lyrically is in the early chapters of *The Breaking of the Image*.[5] Before publication they were delivered as the Gore Lectures given, at that time, in the Jerusalem Chamber at Westminster Abbey (today they have become a single, annual lecture given in the less intimate nave of the Abbey to members of the General Synod). Perhaps it was the extraordinary ambience of that location or perhaps just the challenge of the occasion which inspired the lyricism. Whatever social factors lay behind them, I have long considered them the finest of his writings. Ever the iconoclast, he combines them in the second half of the book with a polemic against liturgical change within the Church of England. The argument is of a piece – namely that the images used within liturgy and worship profoundly shape Christian identity (the first half) and that liturgical changes, which 'are initiated by clerics and defended by them',[6] are in real danger of distorting this identity (the second half). Now, of course, it is perfectly possible to be convinced by the first of these arguments but not the second. Still swimming against the tide, David Martin remains convinced of both, regarding much liturgical change within the Anglican Church as a secularizing factor imposed by the clergy, rather than as a response to popular piety in a context of widespread rejection of traditional liturgical forms. On this we must differ.

Yet, leaving the polemic to one side, liturgical innovators and traditionalists alike can still admire the skilful blend of theological and sociological analysis in the first half of *The Breaking of the Image*. Just to take a single example, he offers an illustration of the way that the cross can become a double

[5] David Martin, *The Breaking of the Image: A Sociology of Christian Theory and Practice* (Oxford: Blackwell, 1980).
[6] Martin, *The Breaking of the Image*, p. 100.

entendre within Christianity. He draws, at this point, on his long-standing fascination with the religious symbols and typologies of war and pacifism, which can be found in his earliest and most recent writings.[7] The cross, for him, is at once a symbol of peace and a symbol of war. There is 'a continuous dialectic whereby the sword turns into the cross and the cross into the sword':

> The cross will be carried into the realm of temporal power and will turn into a sword which defends the established order. It will execute the criminals and heretics in the name of God and the King. But temporal kingship will now be defended by reversed arms, that is a sign of reversal and inversion ... Another illustration ... is provided by the cross which dominates the US Air Force Chapel at Colorado Springs. At the centre of the huge arsenal is a chapel built of stained glass spurs like planes at the point of take-off. The cross is also like a sword. Looked at from another angle the combined cross and sword is a plane and a dove. The plane is poised to deliver death rather than to deliver *from* death and the dove signifies the spirit of peace and concord.[8]

This dialectic understanding of sociology and theology is clearly very different from that of John Milbank in his *Theology and Social Theory*.[9] Martin makes remarkably few references in *Reflections* to other authors – indeed, footnotes become scarcer and scarcer in his books the more recent they become – so when he does it is all the more significant. He has an early reference to Milbank's book which he depicts as 'a recent brilliant study',[10] but then seeks to deconstruct it, albeit without any further explicit mention of it. In the mid-1960s he debated with Bryan Wilson in a very similar manner. If Wilson was the leading British proponent of secularization theory at the time –

---

[7] See David Martin, *Pacifism: An Historical and Sociological Study* (London: Routledge and Kegan Paul, 1965) and *Does Christianity Cause War?* (Oxford: Clarendon Press, 1997).

[8] Martin, *Pacifism*, p. 28.

[9] John Milbank, *Theology and Social Theory: Beyond Secular Reason* (Oxford: Blackwell, 1990); see also his *The Word Made Strange: Theology, Language, Culture* (Oxford: Blackwell, 1997).

[10] Martin, *Reflections*, p. 8.

most notably in his *Religion in Secular Society*[11] – Martin was its leading critic – most notably in his *The Religious and the Secular*.[12] They continued this debate well into the 1970s with very few explicit references to each other's works (the reference that has already been noted from the Preface of *A Sociology of English Religion* is rare). Yet it was clear that they *were* responding to each other and disagreeing with each other. In *Reflections*, Martin uses the same technique to criticize Milbank, arguing at length that the discipline of sociology of religion (which Milbank believes that he has dismissed entirely, albeit without ever mentioning Martin's own work) does help us to understand religious phenomena without reducing them simply to social phenomena. Taking the example of baptism as it is actually practised, he argues that:

> Sociology ... identifies structures, makes comparisons, and formulates, probes and queries from the special viewpoint of orderly curiosity. In the case of baptism nothing is implied about the validity of the faith embodied in baptism. There is simply a widening of interest away from personal involvement towards curious and controlled observation of semi-comparable cases.[13]

The last sentence in this quotation accurately depicts Martin's own role as a sociologist of religion who also happens to be a practising Christian.

In his recent writings there is one major exception to his general practice of criticizing the theories of others through indirect rather than direct means. In his 1997 study *Does Christianity Cause War?* he devotes a whole chapter and several other direct references to the views of Richard Dawkins. He is clearly irritated by the latter's polemic against Christianity and specifically by his contention that 'religion causes wars by generating certainty'.[14] It is not, of course, that Dawkins is a particularly accomplished or well-informed intellectual in the area of religion (see chapter 1). In contrast to some of the

---

[11] Bryan Wilson, *Religion in Secular Society* (London: C. A. Watts, 1966).

[12] David Martin, *The Religious and the Secular* (London: Routledge and Kegan Paul, 1969).

[13] Martin, *Reflections*, p. 10.

[14] Martin, *Does Christianity Cause War?*, p. 22.

continental atheists against whom John Milbank contends at
great length, Dawkins' views on religion are generally delivered
in rhetorical and populist forms. They do not appear to
represent any sustained scholarly study. And yet Dawkins is a
figure of considerable *social* significance. He is the author of
books on evolution that are more widely read by university
students today than any theological books. It is hardly
surprising, in these circumstances, that David Martin, the
believing sociologist, is especially sensitive to this particular
polemic or that he unusually singles Dawkins' views out for such
sustained inspection.

Seeking to exegete the Dawkins claim about war, Martin
argues as follows:

> In one way ... the statement is irrefutable because there
> certainly have been wars where religion played a role. In
> another way it is indefensible since there certainly have been
> wars where religion has played no role whatever. Conflicts
> occur for all kinds of reasons, and hardly ever for just a single
> reason ... Not merely does Dawkins regard religious beliefs
> as childish mistakes which we should learn to grow out of. He
> contends that what is scientifically wrong is at the same time
> morally wrong. So clear a moral judgement may seem
> surprising from the author of *The Selfish Gene*, since in that
> book he indicated a degree of programming for survival
> that might seem to make free will and therefore moral
> judgement otiose.[15]

The critique of Dawkins that Martin offers operates at several
levels. Much of the book operates at a sociological level. Using
one example after another, he seeks to demonstrate that war is
a multivariate phenomenon, sometimes involving religious
institutions and sometimes not. This is probably the easiest of
his tasks and the area at which the Dawkins claim is most
vulnerable. Alongside this there is also a moral critique, as the
final sentence in this quotation indicates. It is indeed one of
the surprising features of Dawkins that he makes such a strong,
almost 'evangelical', attack upon Christianity. There has been
widespread speculation about the sources of his ideological

---

[15] Martin, *Does Christianity Cause War?*, p. 23.

atheism, since it appears so strong and vehement from one who otherwise presents himself as an ideologically free – perhaps even 'value-free' – scientist. David Martin has never been able to resist such obvious moral and ideological dissonances in others. The 'cultured despisers' are undoubtedly cultured but they are also still thoroughly biased despisers. Seventeen years earlier he expressed the hope that the sociologist can perform an important task of ethical commentary in society, especially by analysing ethical decision making independently of those who are actually power holders.[16] In the present critique of Dawkins he observes waspishly at one point that 'Ceausescu would have appreciated at least some of Dawkins's arguments ... [a]rguments which in one context are deployed in the cause of liberality can in another context be used to justify persecution'.[17] And in the quotation above, he allies the role of ethical commentary with sharp observations about the apparent determinism of his writings on evolution.

Thirdly, his critique of Dawkins operates at a theological level:

> In giving an account of the Christian code I tried to lay out the theo-logic and the socio-logic behind the text 'Thy Kingdom comes not by violence.' The Lord tells his servant Peter to 'put up' his sword and explains that his servants do not fight. At the very least, this suggests that Dawkins's theory of the inherent bellicosity of religion is the reverse of what the Gospels actually teach, and Dawkins would need to explain why this is so. There is, after all, not a ghost of a suggestion that the Gospel should be spread by warfare. There is, of course, God's judgement on those who do not recognize the presence of the Kingdom in the imprisoned, the sick, and the beggars, and who do not repent. But nobody is invited to fit out a military expedition to ensure that judgement is enforced here and now. The powers of restitution are entirely eschatological.[18]

---

[16] David Martin, 'Ethical Commentary and Political Decision', *Theology*, LXXVI. 640 (October 1973), pp. 525–31.

[17] Martin, *Does Christianity Cause War?*, p. 75.

[18] Martin, *Does Christianity Cause War?*, p. 163.

Or is this theology? Much of it might just as readily be classified as sociology. As so often in his writings, David Martin slips from one method to another and back again. Ostensibly he writes at a descriptive level here. In reality he is passionately involved and concerned to refute Dawkins. His end to the work makes this abundantly clear:

> If Dawkins's arguments were correct then the separating out of believers and clergy from the general population ought to reveal them as major proponents of violence towards each other and violence in international affairs. This is far from being the case. The evidence does not bear out the contention. The case falls.[19]

To return to *Reflections*, even though few of its ideas are new, the collection does bring together and summarize many of David Martin's long-standing interests. There are, for example, several essays on ecclesiology and ecumenism, all of which demonstrate his continuing independence of thought. Despite remaining the most ecumenical of people in practice, he continues to voice sociological doubts about the limits and politics of ecumenism. David Martin the sociologist is aware that, however desirable greater ecumenism might seem, 'even as ecumenical unions occur among the older bodies, especially in the diaspora, or in countries where they are minorities, new fissures will open up in response to volcanic social upheavals'.[20] Here too the language and not simply the idea of 'fissures' in this context remains after thirty years.

In *Reflections* he also brings together the grand-scale research he has done, first on European churches in *The General Theory of Secularization*[21] in 1978, and then in his recent work on Pentecostalism in South America, first reported in *Tongues of Fire*[22] in 1990. A particularly useful essay in this respect is 'Religious Vision and Political Reality'. His approach to political intervention by churches is cautious. He is convinced that a proper understanding of Christian images should make

[19] Martin, *Does Christianity Cause War?*, p. 220.
[20] Martin, *Reflections*, p. 146.
[21] David Martin, *A General Theory of Secularization* (Oxford: Blackwell, 1978).
[22] David Martin, *Tongues of Fire* (Oxford: Blackwell, 1990).

us suspicious both of political orders *and* of churches as well. Even when Christian beliefs appear to be ambiguously prophetic against particularly egregious political orders, there is a need for some caution. In words that themselves now seem prophetic, he cautions:

> As the Church tangles ambiguously with social processes it will be wise to deploy its weight at the optimum moment, that is, not throw about such weight as it has all the time and explicitly, on one particular side. Even though the circum- stances operative at the optimum moment may require an identification with a particular course or side, as in South Africa, pre-independence Rhodesia, and the Philippines, the Church will probably stand back from that identification as circumstances change, fresh divisions appear, and a newly installed regime exercises power more ambiguously and in its own partial interests.[23]

It is important to note that these words were first delivered as a lecture in Australia in 1986. Two decades later this warning, especially about Zimbabwe and South Africa today, appears to be remarkably accurate. The theologian nurtured on Cranmer's prayers, and alluding to Luther and Kierkegaard, is never sanguine about the propensities of political orders, even those recently liberated from oppressive political regimes. This is not a critique from the political right but rather from a radically theological perspective. The end of the lecture makes this clear:

> Both compromising Church and rigorist monastery or sect pick up continuing impulses from the sharp angle of escha- tological tension set up in the New Testament. If that angle had been less sharp, the warfare of Christian with principal- ities and powers would have been milder, the tension would have been neither stored nor released, and the continuing irony of the Church would not have been available to create guilt in the Christian or dissatisfaction in the outside critic. Of course, the ideal as embodied in the Sermon on the Mount cannot straightforwardly be realized and, in

[23] Martin, *Reflections*, p. 160.

particular, circumstances can motivate Christians to avoid social responsibilities when they should involve themselves in moral ambiguity. Some will argue that this lack of realism is itself not moral: 'the high that proved too high, the heaven for the earth too hard'. But churches exist to raise spires and aspirations, and sect and monasteries exist to protect the dialectic of hope and spiritual autonomy.[24]

That last sentence is characteristically Martin. Even while making a serious and strongly held point, he cannot resist a small piece of word play. In *The Breaking of the Image* there are numerous examples of such word play, even at moments of intense seriousness. Here it is achieved through noting the movements of spires and aspirations.

David Martin has always been a writer who responds well when prompted by specific invitations to give papers. One of the most striking papers in this respect is one he gave in 1995 to a series on 'Harmful Religion' at King's College, London. Although published elsewhere,[25] his paper, entitled 'A Socio-Theological Critique of Collective National Guilt', makes a valuable contribution to *Reflections*. Martin is at his most powerful when he has a fashionable concept to deconstruct. He rose to international fame in the 1960s with his essay 'Towards Eliminating the Concept of Secularisation'.[26] Here he channels his energies into deconstructing the concept of 'collective guilt' and has little difficulty showing the illogicality of expecting individuals to feel guilty about issues for which they can have no personal responsibility. However, this is not simply a semantic quibble. He believes that notions of 'collective guilt' can blunt moral seriousness and (once again) distort liturgies. Theologians should also beware of the distorting effect of such misplaced collective notions:

> In sum, the mistake of Christian utopianism is to conceive the polis as . . . a corporate agent. That mistake represents an

[24] Martin, *Reflections*, p. 161.
[25] In Lawrence Osborn and Andrew Walker (eds.), *Harmful Religion: An Exploration of Religious Abuse* (London: SPCK, 1997).
[26] Published in *The Religious and the Secular* (London: Routledge and Kegan Paul, 1969).

abuse of faith because it attempts simple transfers from the sphere of redemption to the sphere of politics. These transfers themselves damage redemption, turning it into a simplistic programme, which mirrors categories and which shifts the last judgement from the realm of eschatology into a historical possibility. It hands justice over to historians and politicians. Christianity then becomes a mode of secular self-righteousness and denunciation, bypassing the careful assessment of different means of amelioration.[27]

Perhaps it is this sharpness, and occasionally acerbity, which makes David Martin such an enduring and thoughtful critic in both theology and sociology. Within both disciplines he remains an individualist. Amongst sociologists he was instrumental in forcing them to think more clearly about secularization, which had seemed such an obvious force to the founders of modern sociology of religion. Amongst theologians he has been simultaneously a critic of liturgical change and a promoter of a distinctively sociological perspective within theology. I suspect that all of these are areas of debate with much more mileage to come ... not least, I hope, from him. Those of us engaged in these interfaces between theology and sociology remain deeply in his debt.

[27] Martin, *Reflections*, pp. 223–4.

Conclusion

This book has ended acknowledging a long-standing debt and hinting at fresh work yet to be done. Perhaps any work that sets out to explore still-unfolding *changing worlds* is likely to generate as many questions as answers. In all three areas of change studied – moral issues, churchgoing patterns, and theological education – there is much more to be said.

Changing Worlds takes up again some of the moral issues that I studied earlier in *Christian Ethics in Secular Worlds* (1991) and *Moral Leadership in a Postmodern World* (1997). However, there is also at least one major difference. Themes in medical ethics featured in the two earlier books but not in the present one. Ironically, this is because I find that I am increasingly occupied with medical ethics – either sitting on medical ethics committees or giving papers on particular, and usually novel, issues in medical ethics. In the process I have discovered that, even in a supposedly secular world, theologians are genuinely welcome in this context. As the world at large gets ever more pluralist and complex, and as genetic and medical sciences keep uncovering new ethical dilemmas, so voices from faith communities are still valued (provided they do not claim a monopoly of truth and are prepared to listen carefully to others). So, instead of touching on these issues hither and thither in *Changing Worlds*, I plan to return to them more comprehensively at some point in the future.

Changing churchgoing patterns continue to interest and concern me. Since I value worship with others so much in my own life, and indeed enjoy leading worship myself, the study of churchgoing patterns across the world is not simply disinterested academic work. On the contrary, it is intimately linked to my theology and Christian ethics. Some of my secular colleagues have been puzzled at times about why someone so obviously committed to a church should be so interested in studying its apparent demise. In turn, many fellow church-people must consider me to be disloyal for so relentlessly uncovering the extent and scale of churchgoing decline in Britain and many other Western countries. For my part, I regard it as crucial to study changing churchgoing patterns around the world as carefully as possible in order to understand what cannot be changed and what, with appropriate action, might be changed. With so many secular and religious presumptions abounding in this area, I am convinced that careful scholarship is a prerequisite for effective action by churches.

Finally, changing ways of doing theology and of theological education in general require much more thought. The rise of movements such as Christian Virtue Ethics and Radical Orthodoxy has certainly brought a new energy and verve to academic theology. First Stanley Hauerwas and now John Milbank have successfully generated supportive and critical literatures focusing upon their work. Each in his way has also persuaded quite a number of theologians to be more assertive towards their secular colleagues (as well as towards their more liberal theological colleagues). While admiring this energy and verve, I also have some reservations about the agenda it creates. I expressed some of these reservations in *Churchgoing and Christian Ethics* (1999). However, there is more to be done by critics such as myself. It is not enough to be negative: a positive alternative needs also to be developed. There is, I believe, a more open theological tradition – I have sometimes termed it Generous Orthodoxy at and other times Theological Realism – which can learn from secular thought and from other religious traditions while still being embedded in distinctively theological beliefs. Through the series *New Studies in Christian Ethics*, which I have edited for Cambridge University Press over the last decade, a variety of scholars have written on themes within Christian ethics reflecting both this open learning and this theological embedding. Now I believe that it needs to be articulated in theology more widely. This is a challenging task.

INDEX